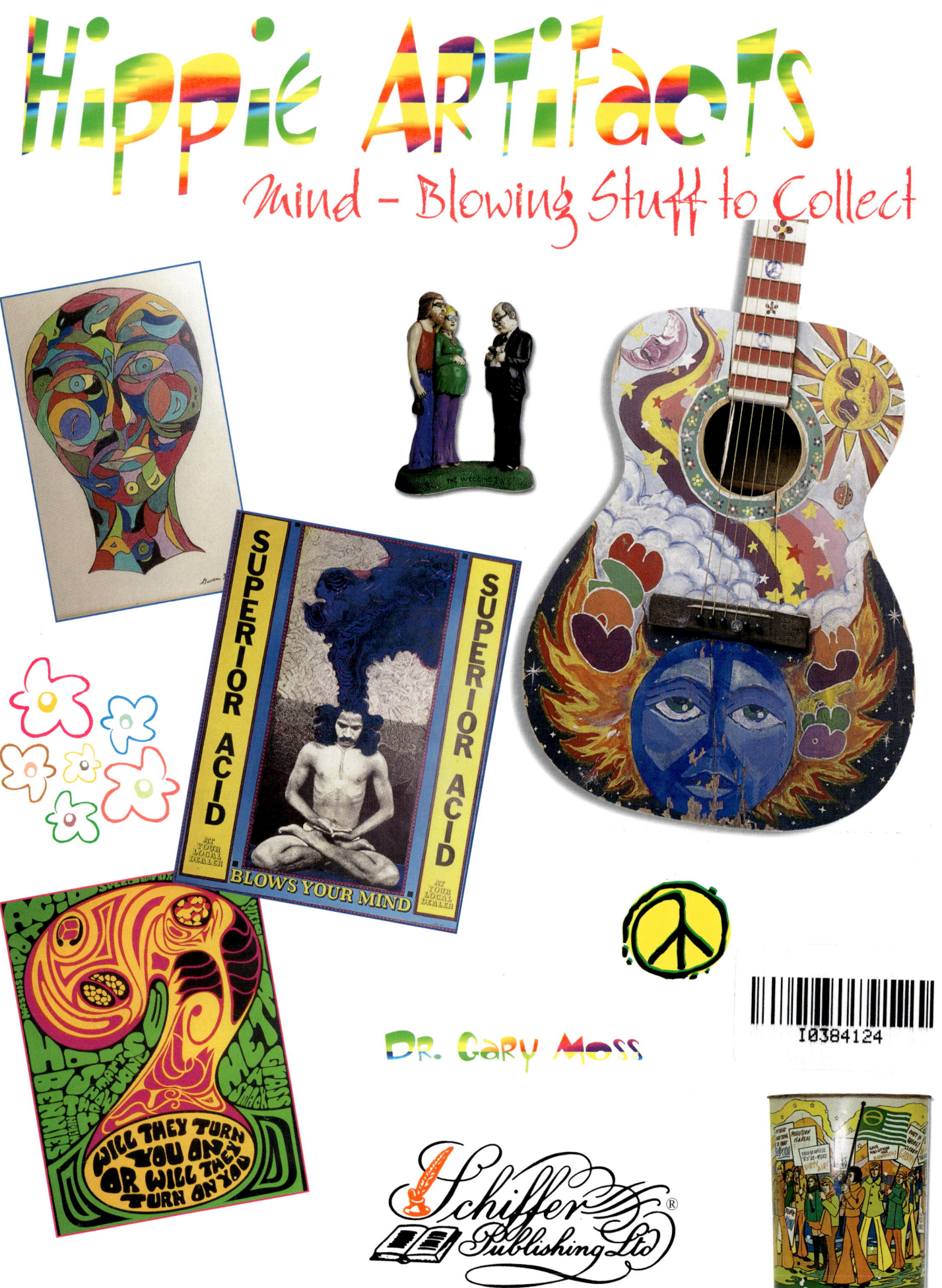

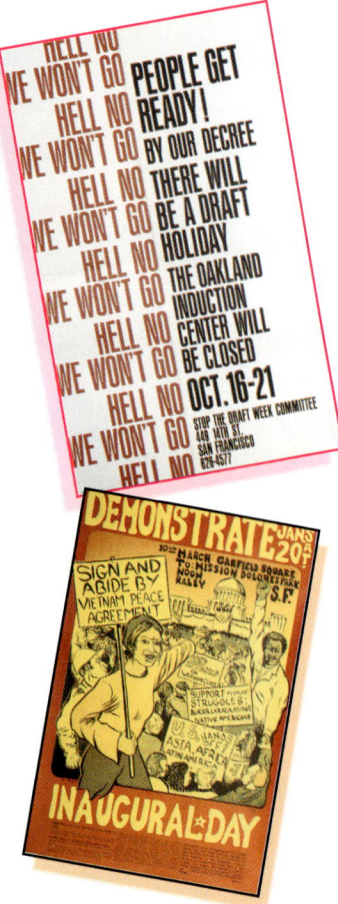

Copyright © 2003 by Gary L. Moss
Library of Congress Control Number: 2002115246

All rights reserved. No part of this work may be reproduced or used in any form or by any means—graphic, electronic, or mechanical, including photocopying or information storage and retrieval systems—without written permission from the copyright holder.

"Schiffer," "Schiffer Publishing Ltd. & Design," and the "Design of pen and ink well" are registered trademarks of Schiffer Publishing Ltd.

Designed by Bonnie M. Hensley
Cover design by Bruce M. Waters
Type set in Ren & Stimpy/Aldine721 BT
ISBN: 0-7643-1758-X
Printed in China
1 2 3 4

Published by Schiffer Publishing Ltd.
4880 Lower Valley Road
Atglen, PA 19310
Phone: (610) 593-1777; Fax: (610) 593-2002
E-mail: Schifferbk@aol.com
Please visit our web site catalog at **www.schifferbooks.com**
We are always looking for people to write books on new and related subjects. If you have an idea for a book, please contact us at the above address.

This book may be purchased from the publisher.
Include $3.95 for shipping.
Please try your bookstore first.
You may write for a free catalog.

In Europe, Schiffer books are distributed by
Bushwood Books
6 Marksbury Avenue
Kew Gardens
Surrey TW9 4JF England
Phone: 44 (0) 20 8392 8585
Fax: 44 (0) 20 8392 9876
E-mail: Bushwd@aol.com
Free postage in the UK. Europe: air mail at cost.

Contents

Acknowledgments	4
Introduction	5
A Little Historical Background	5
A Word About Value	6
Item Availability Rating	6
Chapter One: Peace and Love	7
Peace Man!	7
Love Ya, Baby!	17
Chapter Two: Just BeCAUSE	22
Chapter Three: Jus' Folks: Hand Made Relics	52
Chapter Four: Feeling Groovy: The Drug Culture	72
Chapter Five: Psychedelectibles	91
Chapter Six: Crash Pad	101
Chapter Seven: Flower Power	110
Chapter Eight: Heading in the Right Direction	116
Chapter Nine: Toys and Novelties	124
Chapter Ten: Threads	132
Chapter Eleven: Happenings and Concerts	149
Chapter Twelve: Underground Press	161
Endnotes	176
Bibliography	176

Acknowledgments

The author acknowledges Gary Moise and David Young of the 70s-store.com at Orange Trading Company, Orange, Massachusetts for their contribution of items and information; Gary Sohmers of Wex Rex Collectibles in Hudson, Massachusetts for his contribution of the Buzz Bee; Sterg Zarmakupis, former Manchester, New Hampshire, head shop proprietor, for the gift to the author of the Freak Brothers patch and always an interesting story; the timely and invaluable assistance of Walter "Hawkeye" Potaznick of West Bridgewater, Massachusetts for taking the photographs that were necessary to complete this book; Marek Jacisin of the New England College of Optometry Media Services for producing a few select slides; Marc McGee and the New England College of Optometry Library services; Nikki Slagle for the fine job of editing; Abba Werner for finding some great items, including Dealer McDope; Suzanne White and David Rye for enhancing my poster collection and leading the way with their book; my sister Jamie for her upcoming promotional efforts, and the support of my wife Traudi, and teenage daughters Amber and Blaise. This book is for those for whom the following applies: "If you remember the sixties you weren't really there."

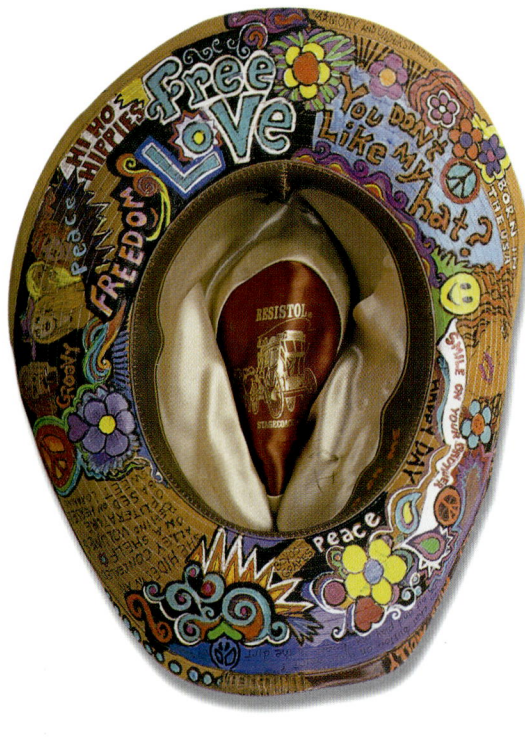

Introduction

The word "hippie," was originally intended to be derogatory, deriving from "hipster" popularized during the late 1950s and early 1960s beatnik era. Beatniks looked down upon the newer counterculture because hippies used drugs simply for the experience rather than a higher artistic aesthetic. The use of the term hippie is first attributed to *San Francisco Examiner* writer Michael Fallon in a 1965 article[1]. In 1966, then governor of California Ronald Reagan described a hippie as someone who "dresses like Tarzan, has hair like Jane, and smells like Cheetah."

For someone with the desire to assemble a new and exciting collection, hippie artifacts are a potential goldmine. Many of the items in this field are currently collected within the boundaries of previously established collectible areas such as vintage clothing, political and protest buttons, rock posters and records, books and magazines, and outsider folk art to name a few. Opportunities exist for a novice collector because the market for many of these items has yet to be established, and a majority of the items that fall within this category are still quite affordable.

Another favorable aspect of this hobby is the likelihood of abundant undiscovered material in attics and basements waiting for a good home. The period of time we are dealing with is only thirty to forty years ago, and there is still tremendous investment potential in many new undiscovered treasures. This is advantageous; many of these items are quite scarce because they were made in limited quantities and were not considered worth keeping.

This book presents a visual history of "collectible items" that were part of the hippie movement, especially in America. It is a socio-anthropologic retrospective of the different facets of hippie life and culture—what motivated, inspired and ultimately destroyed the beliefs to which many young Americans passionately adhered, and the causes that they so vocally supported. It is a pictorial review of their culture and its significant impact on society then and now. One goal is to make the reader aware of the cultural developments of the late 1960s through early 1970s vis-à-vis objects used by this segment of society. The author claims no position on any of the specific issues mentioned, but rather makes awareness of the intrinsic value and rarity of items from this era the subject of the book, and insists he "never inhaled."

A Little Historical Background

During the late 1960s and early 1970s, a major impact on American demographics resulted from the post World War II baby boom. Slightly over half the country was under the age of thirty. This segment of the population became a viable force when expressing its collective opinion on various unresolved and disputed political and social issues of the day, exhibited especially by the motto "sex, drugs, rock n' roll." Between 1965 and 1973, both the East and West Coasts were magnets for young Americans who became disenchanted with traditional conservatism and disillusioned by both conventional politics and increasing American troop presence in Vietnam. A square mile area in San Francisco known as "Haight Ashbury," attracted a growing number of supporters that contributed to the "counter culture revolution." This alternative to mainstream values and behavior included psychedelic drug experimentation, communal living, a return to the land, politically inspired rock music and an interest in Asian religions. Notable West Coast events of that period included Love-ins, Be-ins, Acid Tests, Happenings at Golden Gate Park, and rock concerts at the Fillmore and Avalon Ballrooms.

On the East Coast, New York's East Village, around St. Mark's Place from the East River to Third Avenue and from Houston Street to Fourteenth Street was the primary area for "far out, progressive, activist" music and happenings, underground movie and coffee houses, grass (marijuana) and acid (LSD). This area featured the Balloon Farm, one of the first large warehouse style concert-dance halls to showcase West Coast psychedelic bands as early as 1965. Also notable to this area was the Psychedelicatessen, the first head shop in New York at 10th Street and Avenue A, the protest musical groups the Fugs, David Peel and the Eastside, sexual revolution, folk singers in Washington Park, and a myriad of head shops and underground coffeehouses. These extended into the West Village along Bleecker and McDougal streets. Underground Uplift Unlimited, a major manufacturer of protest buttons, located at 28 St. Mark's Place, across from the Electric Circus and around the corner from Fillmore East, sold buttons, stickers, and posters. The store always stocked hundreds of different political, social and Vietnam protest pins for twenty-five cents each, most of which today sell for ten to thirty-five dollars each and a few select ones reach the one hundred dollar mark.

A Word about Value

What someone is willing to pay for an item at any given time depends upon several factors, including rarity, availability, desirability, condition, and need. The designated range of values for items in this book reflects prices a knowledgeable retail dealer would most likely charge, and a buyer or collector would most likely be willing to pay. The range is for items in near mint condition, meaning very mildly used but not abused. Items in their original sealed packages or boxes may realize significantly higher prices in some instances. Many of the stated values come from dealers, on-line auctions and sales that have occurred. It is always difficult to estimate value for collectibles that do not have a well-established market. For that reason, the author makes no guarantee as to the applicability of the stated prices in all cases, because one or two highly publicized auctions could dramatically influence demand and perception of value. Be aware that several of these items have been reproduced in the decades since the hippie period, and contemporary versions of some items do exist.

Item Availability Rating

I have made a comment for each item about the relative ease or difficulty of finding that item for sale based upon my personal experience and conversations with other collectors and dealers of 60s and 70s memorabilia. "Common" indicates that the item is available, and would be found for purchase at more than one dealer's shop at any given moment or on the Internet within a week's search. Quite often an item in this category is available in dealer inventories as the result of a warehouse find or it was mass-produced and not disposed of during the hippie period. "Uncommon" designates an item that is available, but not typically stocked by dealers, however it does show up for sale several times a year. "Scarce" refers to an item that will occasionally be available, but you may have to wait more than a year to be offered one, or it was made in limited quantity. "Rare" indicates you may have to wait several years before you find an item, and "very rare" is considered almost unique or one-of-a-kind as seen with folk art or hand made items. You may encounter items in these two categories only once or twice every several years, if that. Keep in mind that just because an item is rated "scarce," "rare," or "very rare" does not necessarily mean it is more valuable. It simply denotes how readily available it might be to someone who is in the market to obtain an example. Value and price are also heavily influenced by demand, desirability, and fad appeal in addition to how accessible the item may be to a collector.

Chapter One
Peace & Love

Peace, Man!

Upper left: enamelware teapot with hippie slogans, symbols, and graphics, metal with wood handle, 8" h. x 7" w., c. 1967, very rare, $100-200. *Lower left:* brass hand painted bowl with peace dove, 6" in dia., uncommon, $20-45. *Right:* ceramic peace sign wall plaque, Napcoware, 10" h. x 6" w., 1965, rare, $75-150.

What is now recognized as one of the 1960's most identifiable icons, the peace symbol, actually pre-dates the hippie period by nearly a decade. The Campaign for Nuclear Disarmament, a sponsor of mass marches and sit-downs in London, England, adopted the symbol in 1958. Originally, it stood for "the death of man and the unborn child," but by the mid-1960s it gained universal recognition as a symbol for peace[2]. Many American soldiers referred it to as "the footprint of the great American chicken" during the Vietnam War era[3].

Hawaiian shirt with peace symbol and tapa design, cotton barkcloth, made by Rai Nani, c. 1966, scarce, $75-150.

From left: yellow glossy ceramic peace sign vase, 4" h., rare, c. 1966, $50-100; glass kerosene lamp with peace symbol, Peace Stix, 1969, 10" h., uncommon, $25-45; ceramic peace sign bank, Napcoware, 7" h. x 5" w., scarce, $45-85.

Child's peace shoes, made by Medici. Italian patent leather upper with rubber soles, impressed letters and symbol makes imprint "Children Against the War" in the sand when walking on a beach, c. 1966, very rare, $75-150.

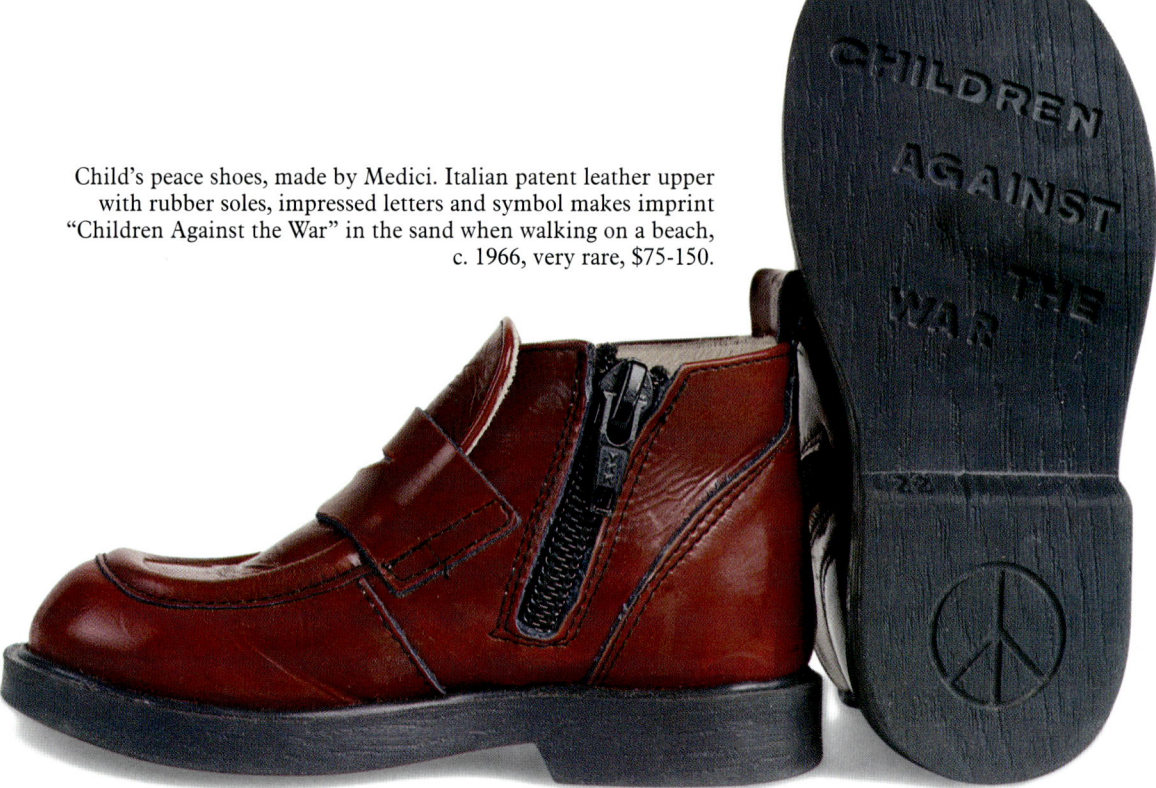

From left: intricately hand tooled and embossed leather peace symbol coin purse, 4" h. x 5" w., very rare, $150-250; *Center:* beaded peace sign head band with leather straps, c. 1967, scarce, $35-65. *Right:* beaded peace sign and rainbow stash bag, 3" h. x 5" w., scarce, $50-85.

Reverse side of leather coin purse showing finger peace sign.

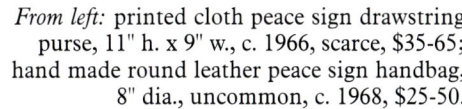

From left: printed cloth peace sign drawstring purse, 11" h. x 9" w., c. 1966, scarce, $35-65; hand made round leather peace sign handbag, 8" dia., uncommon, c. 1968, $25-50.

Center back: plastic serving tray with multicolored peace symbols, 12" dia., uncommon, $15-35. *From left:* plate with peace symbol, 8" dia., c. 1968, common, $10-25; protest button with peace symbol and letters W.D.W.Y.F.W. that stood for popular slogan "we don't want your f*cking war", 2" dia., 1967, uncommon, $15-35; ornate brass peace symbol cuff links, uncommon, $10-25; butane cigarette lighter with "V" for victory peace symbol, common, $10-20; plate with peace symbol, 8" dia., c. 1968, common, $10-25.

The 1960s Peace Movement could be found in a variety of settings. John Lennon and Yoko Ono held "bed-ins" for peace in Amsterdam and Montreal. Several strategies popularized during the late 1960s by hippies and other peace movement advocates were based upon the actions of the British protest group, The Campaign for Nuclear Disarmament. Members of SANE, The Committee for a Sane Nuclear Policy, were often at odds with other anti-war groups because of their stance on peaceful protest.

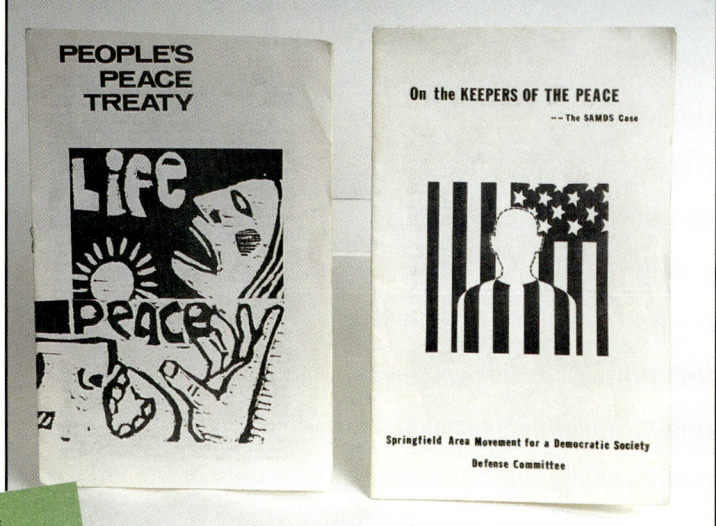

Two eight page pamphlets, printed by Movement Workshop, 8" h. x 5.8" w., Springfield, MA. *From left:* People's Peace Treaty, March 8, 1971, scarce, $35-65; On the KEEPERS OF THE PEACE pamphlet, 1970, uncommon, $25-45.

1973 Peace Calendar, published by War Resister's League, New York, rare, $45-85.

Metal peace symbol necklace pendants, sold in head shops for several years, larger more ornate 3"-4" dia. pendants as pictured are uncommon, $10-25, smaller 1"-2" dia. plain pendants are common, $5-15.

Left: Little Prince Peace Plaque, Christmas tree hanging light, 7" dia., Stanwell Trading Co., originally sold for $2.96, rare, $75-150. *Upper right:* clear blue drinking glass, and milk glass coffee mug, both common, $5-10. *Lower right:* metal peace sign electric wall clock with thin clear celluloid cover, Lendan, 12" dia., c. 1968, scarce, $50-100.

Garry Knox Bennett, selling peace symbols and roach clips to head shops on Haight Street, started Squirkenworks. He states: "Thank God for hippies…You could sell them anything."[4]

Lighted peace symbol for mounting on the inside of rear automobile window, plastic, V&M Enterprises, Mt. Clemens, MI, 4.5" dia., uncommon, $20-45.

Metal hood ornament, 4" dia., made by Ghia Products Group, 1968, uncommon, $15-35.

From left: peace sign wristwatch, Swiss made, original leather strap with metal anchors, scarce, $35-65; silver peace symbol charm, Squirkenworks, San Francisco, scarce, $15-35.

From top: enamel peace sign cufflinks, 1.5" dia., common, $10-20; Murano glass trade bead and leather choker, 1969, 16" long, uncommon, $35-65; decorative enamel brass "love" necklace, three 1" squares with psychedelic design, uncommon, $25-45; red, white and blue leather peace sign hair barrette, c. 1968, common, $5-10.

Top row: four different metal and brass rings, c. 1965-72, common, $5-15. *Center from left:* abalone and metal bracelet, uncommon, $15-35; abalone cuff links, uncommon, $10-25. *Bottom from left:* Squirkenworks silver charm; miniature butane lighter, 0.5" h. c. 1966, uncommon, $15-35.

Rear from left: telephone/address hardbound booklet with multiple peace symbol cover decor, 10" h. x 4" w., c. 1967, uncommon, $15-35; red wax candle with embossed peace symbol, 7" h. x 4" w., uncommon, $10-25; peace symbol necktie, cotton, uncommon, $10-25; peace loving man novelty joke box, 1970, common, $5-15. *Front from left:* leather belt with attached metal peace symbols, scarce, $35-65; white vinyl belt with silver peace sign buckle, c.1967, uncommon, $25-50; brass peace sign belt buckle, common, $10-20.

From left: clear vinyl pillow with hand peace sign, 11" square, c. 1966, uncommon, $20-45; *Popstickles*, decorative stick-on for telephones, Dal Mfg. Corp., Providence, RI, 12" h. x 9" w., c. 1968, common, $5-15.

Silk scarf with red, white and blue multiple peace symbol motif, c. 1966, uncommon, $15-35.

From top: cut and pressed tin and aluminum bracelets and brooch, c. 1965-72, common, $10-20; enamel swirl décor bracelet with stamped peace signs, c. 1967, scarce, $35-65; pot metal heart shaped enamel hair barrette, common $5-10 (post hippie period); leather and brass peace bracelet, common, $10-20.

Hang-Um-Up paper peace mobiles, Allied Paper Corp., 14" dia., c. 1966, uncommon, $10-25 each.

Leather stick-on peace symbol for jackets and jeans, uncommon, $10-20.

Assorted peace sign paper and cloth patches, c. 1965-72, common, $5-15 each.

Top row from left: Realistic peace transistor radio, 6" dia., 1968, scarce, $35-65; jacket and jeans cloth trim with embroidered doves, peace sign, male and female symbols, uncommon, $10-25; NECK-ERS dog collar style beaded choker with hanging peace symbol, c. 1969, scarce, $35-65. *Bottom row from left:* glassine Christmas tree bulb with frosted dove and peace sign, c. 1965, uncommon, $5-15; brass belt buckle with hand peace sign, common, $10-20; slip-on hammered metal bracelet with attached hippie symbols, 1.5" w., c. 1967, uncommon, $20-45; red, white and blue salt and pepper dispenser with black embossed peace symbol, plastic, 1966, uncommon, $5-15.

Beach towel with graphic images of various hippies, peace and love signs, uncommon, cotton, c. 1968, uncommon, $10-25.

Top row from left: ceramic hexagon shaped bank with peace sign, 5" h. x 5" w., uncommon, $20-45; Peace, a committed jig-saw puzzle, American Publishing Corp., 1969, common, $10-20; wood carved hand peace sign, value depends on size, smaller than 8" are common, $10-20, from 8"-16" are uncommon, $20-45, and 16" plus are scarce, $45-95. *Bottom row from left:* Dura-lite light bulb with peace symbol filament in original package, uncommon, $15-35, value is 50% higher with paper package; metal beer can shaped light fixture with peace sign, 1968, uncommon, $25-50, value is 50% less without bulb; painted wax candle "See the Light" in the shape of a light bulb with peace sign, rare, $50-100; black-light lamp with peace sign ceramic base, scarce, $50-100, value is 50% less without bulb.

The peace sign pin in the form of a B-52 bomber with the words "Drop It" could refer to opposite viewpoints. One reference could be to "drop the war" while another could be "drop the bomb" because B-52s were used for carpet-bombing in North Vietnam.

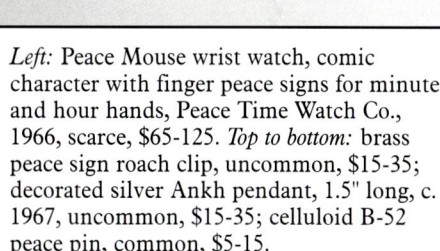

Left: Peace Mouse wrist watch, comic character with finger peace signs for minute and hour hands, Peace Time Watch Co., 1966, scarce, $65-125. *Top to bottom:* brass peace sign roach clip, uncommon, $15-35; decorated silver Ankh pendant, 1.5" long, c. 1967, uncommon, $15-35; celluloid B-52 peace pin, common, $5-15.

Sleeping bag with psychedelic and flower power motif, the word Peace throughout the artwork, c. 1968, uncommon, $25-50.

Peace NOW poster, designed by H. Getladt and K. Marsh, a winning poster design from a 1966 Avant-Garde magazine contest, 29" h. x 23" w., rare, $100-250.

Peace poster titled "the white dove" with row of police confronting row of hippies, designer Dean Eller of Kenrick Associates, Indianapolis, 26" h. x 22" w., 1970, scarce, $75-150.

Love Yah, Baby!

From left: metal LOVE electric wall clock with thin clear celluloid cover, Lendan, 12" dia., c. 1968, scarce, $50-100; cloth and vinyl op art design LOVE handbag, 14" h. x 18" w., scarce, $45-85; enameled metal LOVE ashtray, 8" sq., c. 1966, uncommon, $15-35.

After Robert Indiana created his classic "LOVE" design, many commercial and decorator items were produced using a similar concept. Robert Indiana was born in 1928 and became a leader of the Pop Art movement in America. His legacy includes color lithographic images depicting significant topics of the 1960s and 1970s avant-garde movement in America. His best-known image, "LOVE" became an icon of the peace movement. Many of his designs were incorporated into items made by Fritz & Floyd of Dallas Texas, often marked with an "FF Japan" paper label on the bottom of the item.

Novelty LOVE wristwatch with eyes that move back and forth denoting seconds. Made by Sega, Israel, original flicker wristband, 1969, scarce, $50-100.

From left: vinyl blow-up floor pillow with LOVE and peace dove, 16" square, Dan-Dee Imports, New York, 1970, scarce, $25-50; LOVE butane cigarette lighter, c. 1966, common, $10-20; telephone address book, 10" h. c. 1967, uncommon, $10-20; LOVE pendant, 3" h. c. 1967, common, $10-20; hardbound book, *Love Lyrics*, Louis Untermeyer, Odyssey Press, New York, 1965, common, $5-10.

From left: plastic designer Italian sunglasses with rainbow coated lenses that spell LOVE in a psychedelic style, c. 1967, rare, $45-85; boxed set of interchangeable colored lenses for round metal eyeglass frame, Chameleon, c. 1969; wearer could change eyeglass lens color to match their mood, scarce, $35-65.

Left and right: ceramic hippie girl penny banks, 6" h. x 4" w., uncommon, c. 1968, $25-50. *Center:* enamel tray with floral design and LOVE, 14" dia., c. 1967, uncommon, $15-35; glass ashtray with LOVE transfer, 6" dia., c. 1967, uncommon, $15-35.

Silk scarf with op art LOVE design, 22" square, c. 1967, uncommon, $15-35.

Rear from left: LOVE pillow, 10" dia., applied letters, c. 1968, common, $10-25; set of four LOVE drinking glasses with original cardboard holder, Anchor Hocking, 1967, common, single glass, $5-10, complete set of 4 with holder, $50-100. *Front from left:* highly decorative LOVE transferware coffee mug with psychedelic design by Pia, 5" h. 1968, scarce, $25-45; realistic transistor LOVE radio, 6" dia., 1968, scarce, $35-65.

Hang-Um-Up paper LOVE mobiles, Allied Paper Corp., 14" dia., c. 1966, uncommon, $10-25 ea.

From top: leather hand tooled and painted LOVE bracelet, common, $10-20; leather LOVE choker, 16" long, common, $5-15; "LOVE is happening" pinback, 2" dia., celluloid c. 1967, common, $5-10; cloth embroidered LOVE earrings, common, $5-10 (post hippie period); leather LOVE choker, 16" long, common, $5-15.

Sleeping bag with psychedelic and flower power motif, the word LOVE throughout the artwork, c. 1968, uncommon, $20-45.

From left: cloth lampshade, 20" dia., 1968, scarce, $25-50; Love Bead Jewelry set, Walcrafts, Inc., c. 1968, common, $10-25; Red leather belt with mirrored cutout heart design, 1968, uncommon, $20-45; Peter Max "Love," metal tray, uncommon, $35-65; Love Photo Frame, Dan-Dee Import, 4" square, 1971, common, $10-20.

Beach towel "Make Love Not War" with psychedelic and flower power graphics, c. 1967, uncommon, $10-25.

Leather saddle shoes with peace symbol and Love, Peterman Shoes, c. 1966, rare, $50-100. *Photograph courtesy of Walter "Hawkeye" Potaznick, West Bridgewater, MA.*

Chapter Two
Just be CAUSE

Many extremist groups evolved in the late 1960s as vocal and visible catalysts of change. However, several of these factions became so militant that they alienated even the most ardent of their grass roots supporters. Better known groups of the period include the Black Panthers, the Weathermen, the Yippies, the Chicago Seven, and the Catonsville Nine. Visionaries represented by Women's Liberation, Gay and Lesbian Advocacy and Global Ecological Awareness created longer lasting movements. The caustic and incendiary mood of the period was characterized in the lyrics of the song "Eve Of Destruction" written by P.F. Sloan and recorded by Barry McGuire for Dunhill Records: *"The Eastern world it is explodin', violence flarin' and bullets loadin'. You're old enough to kill, but not for votin'. You don't believe in war, but what's that gun you're totin'?"* This 1965 song, banned from the airwaves in several cities due to the inflammatory nature of the lyrics, was popular during the early days of the hippie protest period.

Rally against the war and racism poster, "Demonstrate Inaugural Day Sat Jan 20", designed by R.K.M., 18" h. x 12" w., 1972, very rare, limited distribution, $200-400.

Satirical antiwar vacation poster, 35" h. x 23" w., c. 1966, common, $25-45.

Socialist Worker's party 1970 handbill, advocating an end to American troops in Viet Nam, 3" h. x 5.5" w. This was a non-presidential voting year; probably used by congressional candidates, common, $10-20.

Draft protest T-shirt with satiric theme for the U.S. Selective Service System, using a "peace" dove instead of the American eagle (representing the government war effort) c. 1968, rare, $50-100.

Booklet, *Germ Warfare Research for Viet Nam*, published by Philadelphia area Committee to End the War in Viet Nam, 30 pages, 1966, scarce, $25-45.

Anti war rally poster, "If Everyone Read This Poster…," published by the Committee for the Fall Offensive, 20" h. x 12" w., 1969, scarce, $100-250.

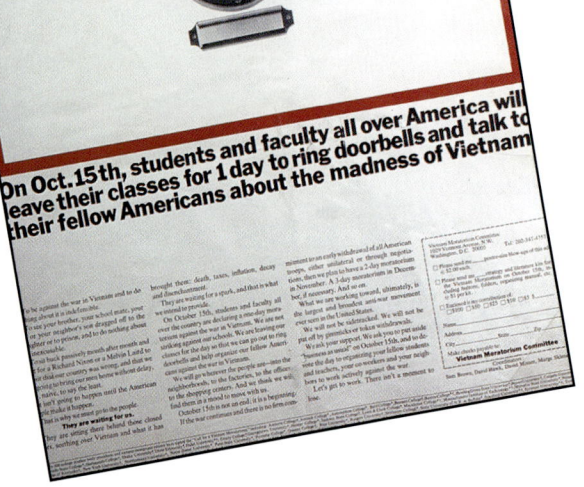

Poster, "Press Button to End War," published by Viet Nam Moratorium Committee, 32" h. x 22" w., 1966, scarce, $100-250.

Propaganda booklet, *Viet Nam Will Win*, 47 pages, published by Peoples Press, 11" h. x 8" w., 1969, scarce, $50-100.

Anti-war poster, "Chicken Little Was Right," printed by Prints, Norristown, PA, 36" h. x 24" w., 1969, uncommon, $25-45. *Photograph courtesy of Walter "Hawkeye" Potaznick, West Bridgewater, MA.*

Poster, National Student Moratorium May 5th..., printed by Student Mobilization Committee, West Coast office, 22" h. x 17"w., scarce, $100-250.

The clenched fist, originally used by European Socialists and Communists, symbolized "power to the people." The Black Panthers and other radical student groups adopted it as their symbol.

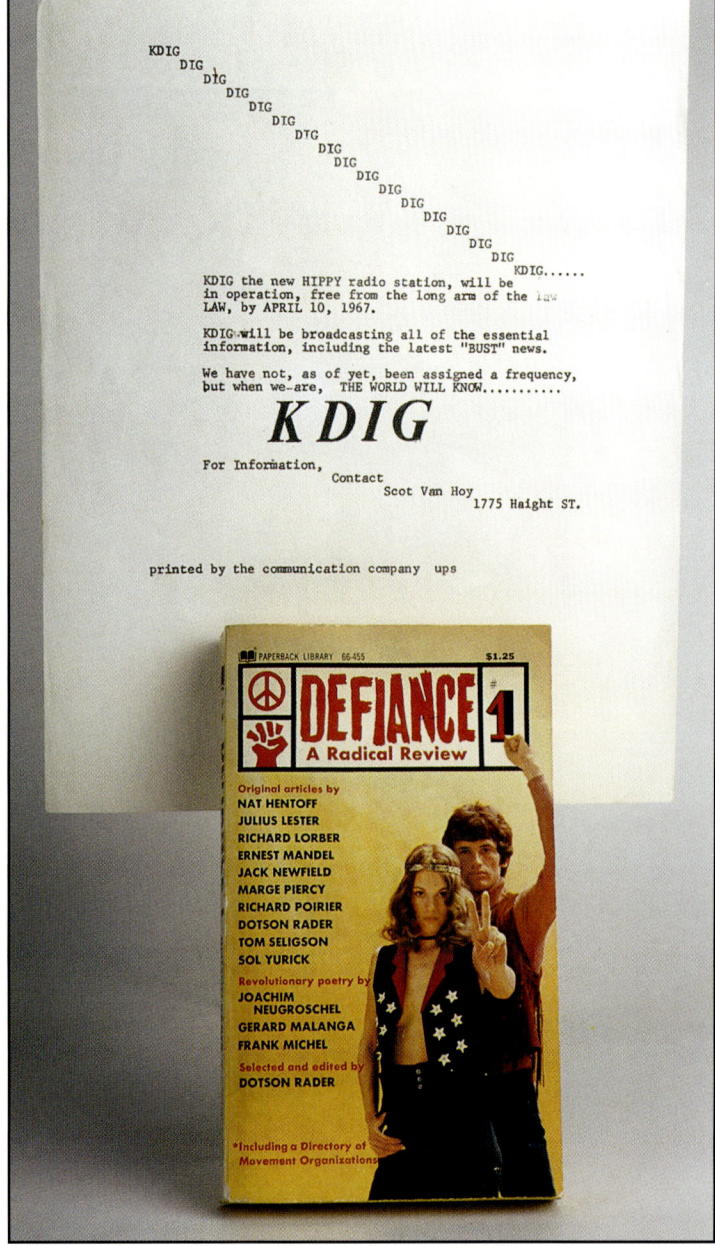

From top: handbill announcing "the new Hippy radio station KDIG will be in operation free from the long arm of the LAW, by April 10, 1967," and reporting all the latest "BUST" news, 1775 Haight St., San Francisco, 11" h. x 8.5" w., rare, $35-65; book, *Defiance, A Radical Review #1*, edited by Dotson Rader, Paperback Library, New York, October 1970, common, $5-10.

The "Great Society" was President Lyndon Johnson's motto used in a May, 1964 speech in which he proposed an American society free of poverty and prejudice, giving everyone the opportunity to have a fulfilling, happy lifestyle. Using a similar message, Eugene McCarthy's presidential bid in 1968 was based upon the antiwar sentiment of the grass roots peace movement. Many of his volunteers were young people that used the slogan "Clean for Gene." McCarthy's increasing popularity forced Lyndon Johnson to back out of the Democrat Primary in 1968 allowing Johnson's pro-war Vice-President Hubert Humphrey to enter the race and become the nominee of the volatile Democratic National Convention in Chicago, marred by violent police confrontation with anti-war protesters. Anti-Humphrey protests gained momentum from March through November of 1968, resulting in Humphrey's loss to the Republican candidate, Richard Nixon.

Cork dartboard with image of President Lyndon Johnson in original package, Arthur Naiman, Grand Central Sta., New York, 10" dia., 1966, scarce, $35-65.

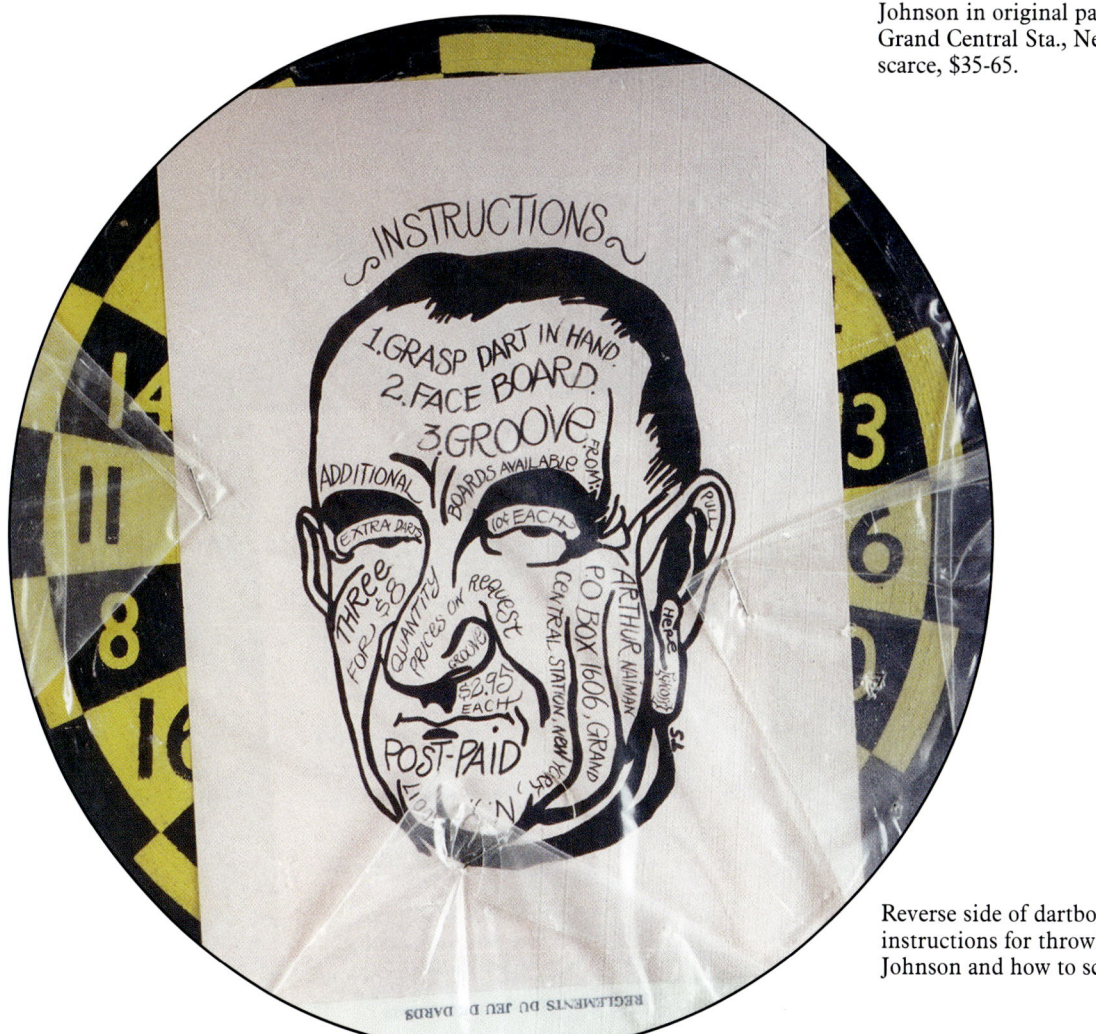

Reverse side of dartboard, politically satirical instructions for throwing darts at Lyndon Johnson and how to score.

Richard Nixon won the 1968 presidential campaign with a promise to end U.S. military involvement in Vietnam. The anti-war movement initially occupied universities. However, when the American death toll began to rise and news about the Tet offensive became known, many Americans previously on the sideline began to oppose the war. President Nixon and his Secretary of State Henry Kissinger were determined to "save face," choosing to expand troop presence into Cambodia and Laos. This greatly accelerated protests around the country including one at Kent State University in Ohio where, on May 4, 1970, national guardsmen killed four students.

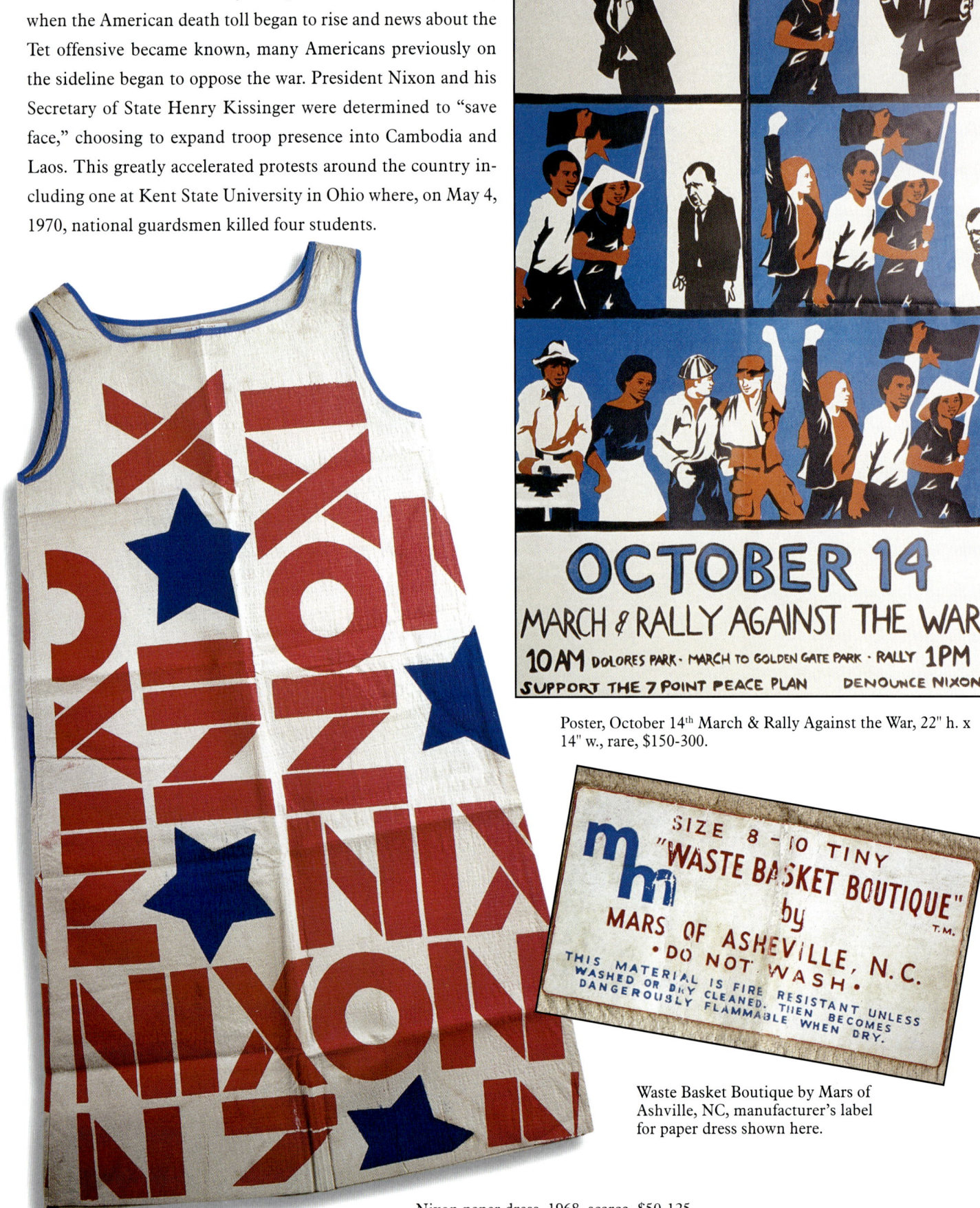

Poster, October 14th March & Rally Against the War, 22" h. x 14" w., rare, $150-300.

Waste Basket Boutique by Mars of Ashville, NC, manufacturer's label for paper dress shown here.

Nixon paper dress, 1968, scarce, $50-125.

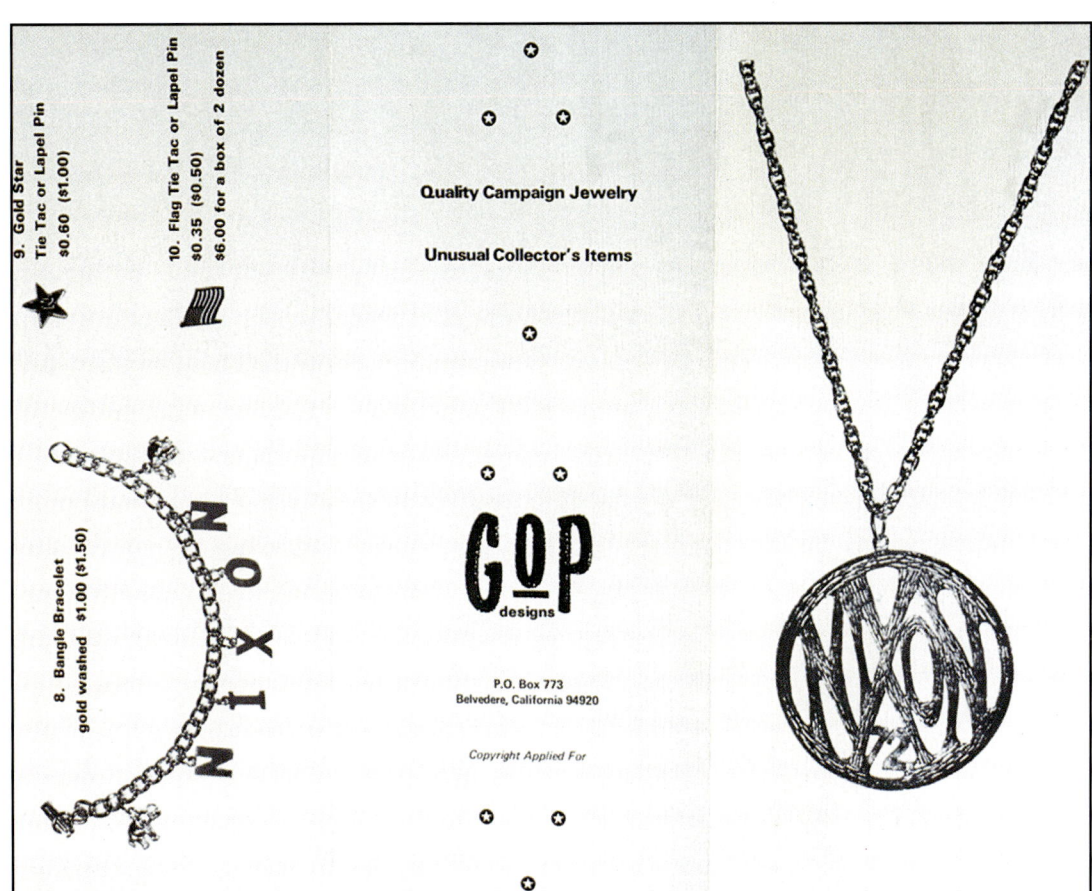

Tri-fold brochure for Nixon re-election jewelry showing use of popular hippie design necklace used to attract young voters, GOP Designs, Belvedere, CA, 11" h. x 4" w., 1972, scarce, $20-45.

From left: puzzle, "Who Can Beat Nixon," 1970, uncommon, $20-50; Nixon protest T-shirt using a swastika to replace the "x" in Nixon, 1970, scarce, $35-65; Nixon blow-up punching bag, 1970, uncommon, $25-45. *Collection courtesy of Gary Moise, 70's-store.com at Orange Trading Company, Orange, MA.*

Satirical anti-Nixon poster, "Bring Us Together," pictures Nixon as a hippie, artist Omar, printed by Kennedy Studio, Boston, 34" h. x 22" w., 1969, uncommon, $45-85.

Satirical anti-Nixon poster, "Bring Us Together #2," pictures Nixon as a gladiator, artist Omar, printed by Kennedy Studio, Boston, 34" h. x 22" w., 1969, uncommon, $45-85.

In order to insure that he won the 1972 presidential election, Nixon ordered his closest aides to bug the phones at Democratic National headquarters in the Washington D.C. Watergate building. However, on June 17, 1972, seven men were caught and charged with breaking and entering. All the men at the time were working for CREEP (The Campaign To Re-Elect The President).

Watergate poster #767, artist: Ralph Reese, black light effect, printed by Third Eye Inc., New York, 35" h. x 22" w., 1973, scarce, $75-150.

Guerilla, volume 2, number 3, San Francisco, 1968, "published occasionally as a broadside of poetry and revolution", a free cultural supplement of the Liberation News Service for the Black Panther Party, promotes "Revolution" and "Eldridge Cleaver, Minister of Information/Black Panther Party, for President". Quote on front reads "Our purpose in entering the political arena is to send the jackass back to the farm and the elephant back to the zoo," an obvious reference to the Democratic and Republican parties, 22" h. x 16" w., very rare, $100-250.

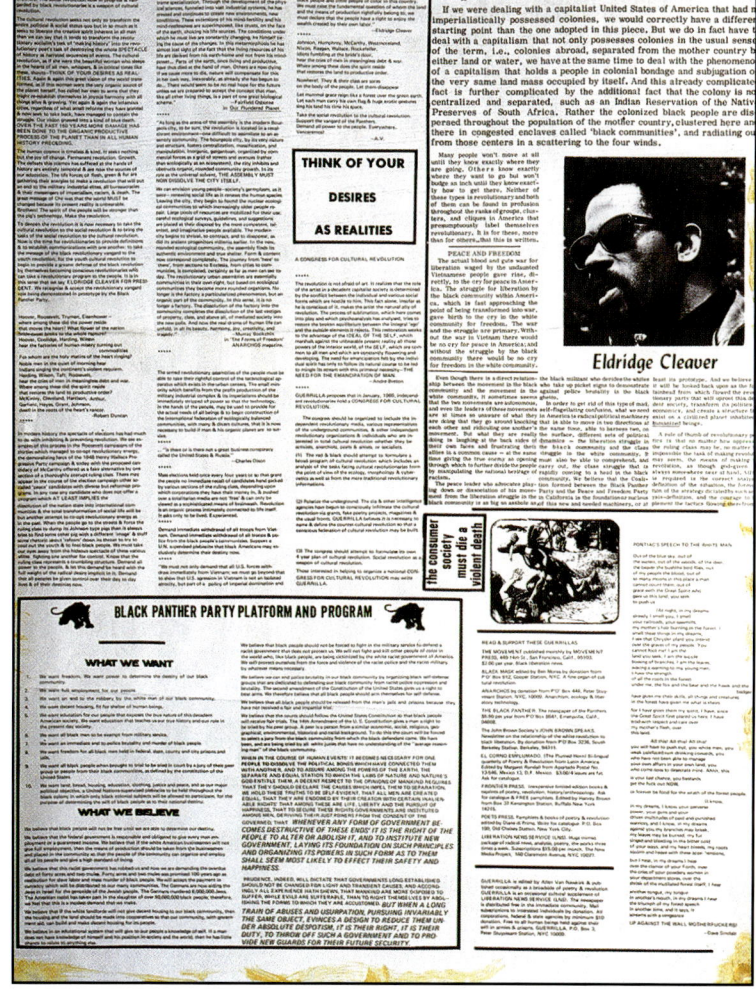

Reverse side of *Guerilla* features articles about the black power movement, the plight of Afro-Americans, Black Panther Party platform and program, including quote that reads "The spirit of the people will be stronger than the pig's technology."

The Black Panther Party was formed in Oakland, California in October 1966. Originally, it was a militant group advocating black self-defense and the restructuring of American society based on increased social, political, and economic equality for African-Americans. The founding members, Huey Newton and Bobby Seale, first attracted attention in May 1967 at a protest march against a bill under consideration that would outlaw carrying loaded weapons in public. Marchers wearing distinctive black leather jackets and black berets gathered at the California state capitol in Sacramento armed with weapons. The extensive national media news coverage given to the event led to the formation of Black Panther chapters outside the San Francisco Bay area. Chapters eventually spread throughout the country. Eldridge Cleaver led the Panther's "Free Huey" movement after Newton was arrested in October 1967 and charged with murdering a police officer in Oakland. Cleaver became a Black Panther Party leader and in 1968, the presidential candidate from the anti-war Peace and Freedom Party. Stokely Carmichael, who was president of the Student Nonviolent Coordinating Committee in 1966, is credited with coining the term "Black Power."

From left: afro hair pick with clenched fist and original package, 8" h. x 3.5" w., 1967, common, $10-20; carved mahogany clenched fist, 9" h. x 5" w. c. 1967, scarce, $50-100. *Collection courtesy of Gary Moise, 70's-store.com at Orange Trading Company, Orange, MA.*

The East Village Other, v1, n18, Aug 15-Sep 1, 1965, underground newspaper with lead article "Black Power in the Ghetto," common, $10-25. Early issues and front cover images have greatest effect on value.

Left rear: hard bound book non-fiction *Black Power Revolt*, edited by Floyd Barbour, published by Extending Horizons Books, Boston, 1968, common, $5-15. *Right rear:* Black Panther Party propaganda pamphlet, *The Genius of Huey Newton*, published by The Ministry of Information, 1970, uncommon, $35-65. *Center:* propaganda pamphlet of the Afro-American Liberation Army Party, a black militant guerilla army, *Humanity, Freedom, Peace*, published by the Revolutionary Peoples Communication Network, 1969, scarce, $50-100. *Front from left:* 1.25" Black Panther pin and 1.25" Bobby Seale pinback, 1967, uncommon, $25-50; color variations or local chapter markings have added interest and value. "Black Power" pinback, 3" dia., uncommon, $10-25.

Angela Davis entered the national spotlight after being removed from the faculty of UCLA because of her membership and Vice Presidential candidacy in the Communist Party. She was a suspect in the August 7, 1970 conspiracy to free George Jackson during his trial in Marin County, California, and placed on the FBI's 10 Most Wanted List. After serving sixteen months in prison, she was acquitted.

Angela Davis, Vice Presidential Candidate, Communist Party USA, speaking in Student Union Ballroom, University of Massachusetts, Amherst, Sat. April 12th, 23" h. x 19" w., 1967, scarce, $75-175.

Malcolm X, born Malcolm Little, learned about the teachings of Islam while in prison for robbery. He joined the Nation of Islam under the leadership of Elijah Muhammad, and upon his release, preached black superiority and race separation to attain equality. In 1964, he started the Organization of Afro-American Unity, which pledged to promote greater harmony among all nationalities and races. He was shot and killed on February 22, 1965, while giving a speech in the Harlem Ballroom.

From left: news service photo of black marchers, 1965, Boston, MA, 8" h. x 10" w., uncommon, $10-25; booklet, *Malcolm Talks to Young People*, professing the philosophy of the black power struggle through the thoughts of Malcolm X, common, $5-15.

Joan Baez started the Institute for the Study of Non-Violence. She refused to appear on the popular television show *Hootenanny* because the show previously refused to showcase certain performers with liberal political views.

Handbill for war resisters in need of draft or military counseling, lists referral sources and sanctuary churches in San Francisco Bay area, 14" h. x 10" w., very rare, $50-150.

Reverse side of handbill, photo of folksinger and anti-war activist Joan Baez, founder of "The Institute for the Study of Non-Violence in 1965," photo credit Bob Fitch.

In January 1966, President Lyndon Johnson eliminated student deferments from the draft, increasing student resentment about the war in Vietnam. The Students for a Democratic Society (SDS), a driving political force on many college campuses throughout the 1960s, began in Chicago in 1962. The SDS saw the increased antiwar sentiment as an opportunity to ignite a united student movement. As a result, hundreds of new SDS chapters were formed on campuses across the country. One of the better known slogans used by the SDS was "Make Love, Not War." The SDS organized draft-card burnings including one in New York's Central Park in 1969, called the Spring Mobilization to End the War in Vietnam, attracting half a million antiwar protesters. Chanting, "Burn cards, not people," and "Hell no, we won't go!" hundreds of young men threw their draft cards into a large bonfire.

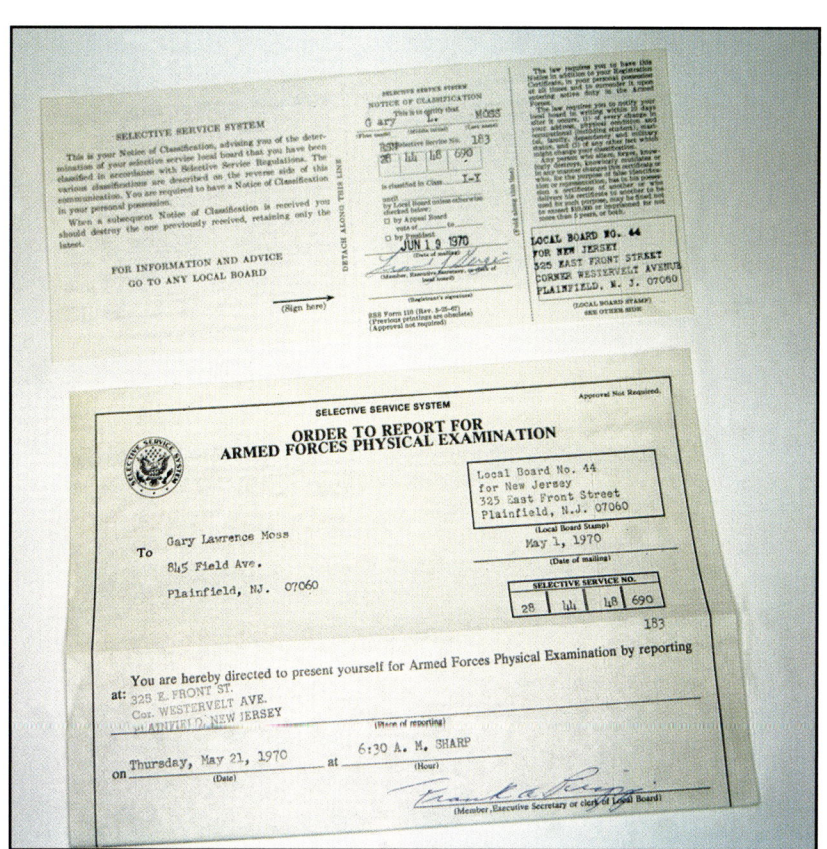

From top: author's Selective Service draft card, classification I-Y (qualified for military service only in time of war or national emergency); these were ceremonially burned at anti-war rallies by draft resisters, 1970, scarce; author's Order to Report for Armed Forces Physical Examination. Notices of this nature prompted great amounts of stress as well as creativity in the seventeen to twenty-five year old American male, 1970, scarce, value difficult to determine. *Photograph courtesy of Walter "Hawkeye" Potaznick, West Bridgewater, MA.*

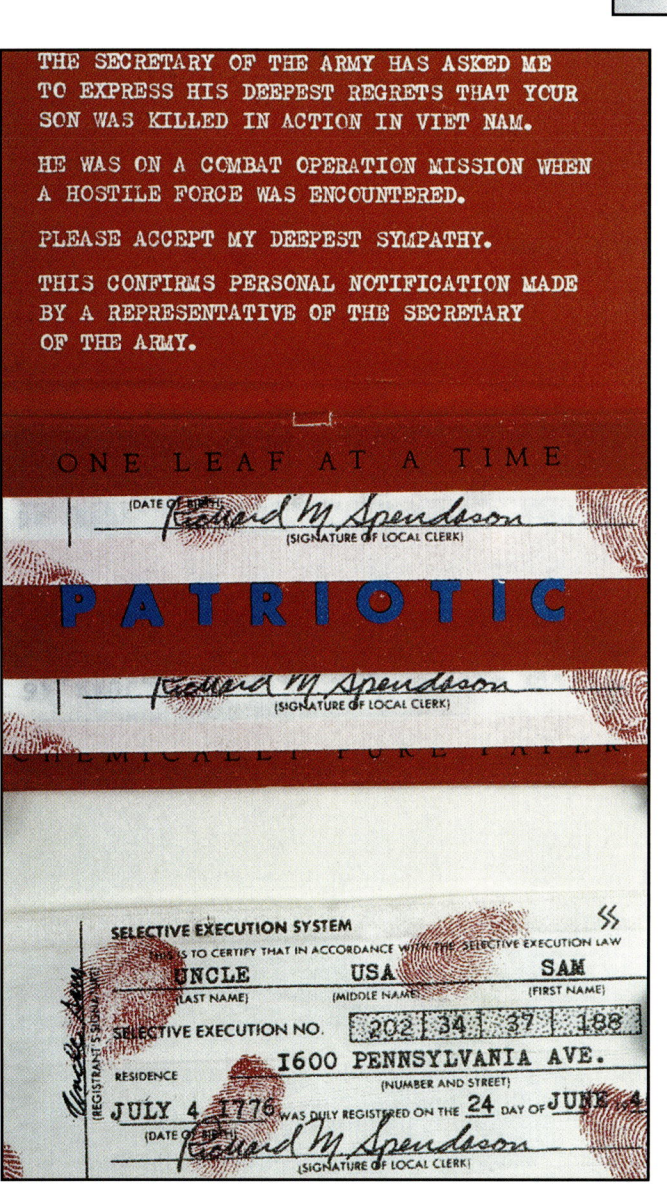

Cigarette rolling papers using facsimile image of a draft card, "selective execution system," inside pack cover informs reader that their "son was killed in action in Viet Nam," 1970, uncommon, $15-35.

HELL NO WE WON'T GO *(repeated)*

PEOPLE GET READY!

BY OUR DECREE THERE WILL BE A DRAFT HOLIDAY

THE OAKLAND INDUCTION CENTER WILL BE CLOSED

OCT. 16-21

STOP THE DRAFT WEEK COMMITTEE
449 14TH ST.
SAN FRANCISCO
626-4577

Draft protest poster, "Hell No We Won't Go," announcing a draft holiday and close of the Oakland induction center for one day, printed by Berkeley Graphic Arts, 20" long, 14" w., 1966, very rare, $100-250.

Another anti-war incident three years later involved the unprovoked shooting by Ohio National Guardsmen of four students at Kent State University on May 4, 1970. This tragic event was immortalized in the Neil Young song "Ohio" that includes the lyrics "... *four dead in Ohio.*"

Handbill announcing a march and rally commemorating the first year anniversary of the killing of four students at Kent State University in Ohio by national guard troops and protesting American troop presence in Cambodia, 11" h. x 8.5" w., 1971, uncommon, $25-45.

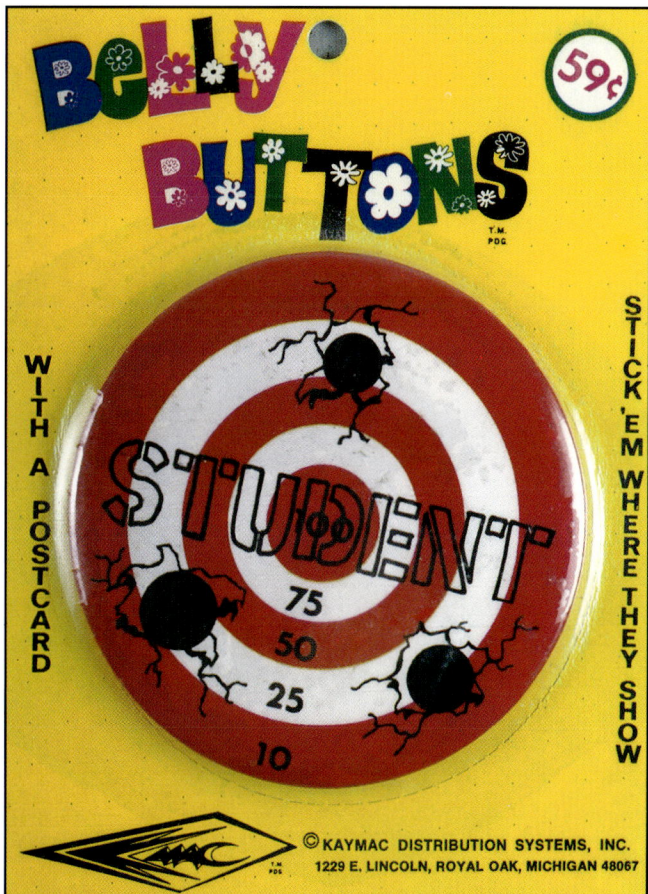

Belly Buttons, 3" dia. pinback on a mailing postcard, an obvious reference to the killing of four students at Kent State in Ohio in May 1970, Kaymac Distribution Systems, Royal Oak, MI, scarce, $35-65.

Photographic poster collage of Syracuse University anti-war protesters during the late 1960s, 22" h. x 18" w., 1968, scarce, $100-175.

Handbook, *Keeping Your Cool in a Civil Disturbance*, 6" h. x 4" w., 1971, scarce, $25-45.

Inside page of *Civil Disturbance* handbook showing a "hippie chick" distracting a soldier during a protest rally by lifting up her shirt.

Inside page of *Civil Disturbance* handbook showing a "hippie guy" inciting a soldier during a protest rally by giving him the finger.

May Day Manual, "Power to the People," 14 page mimeographed booklet describing what to do in a protest march when confronted by the authorities, 11" h. x 8.5" w., 1971, rare, $50-150.

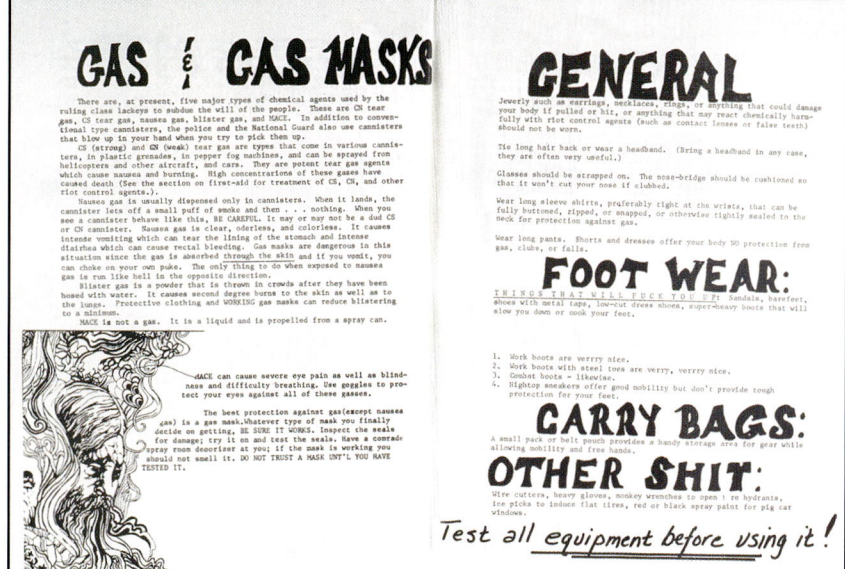

Inside page of *May Day Manual*, explaining what to wear and what to do if tear gassed during a protest march.

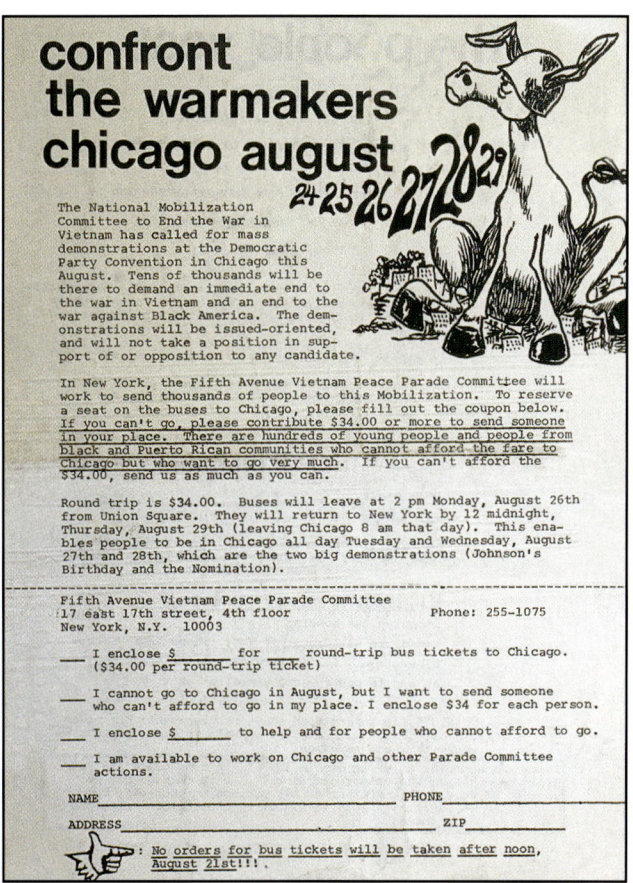

Handbill "Confront the War Makers," Chicago, August 25-28, printed by Fifth Avenue Vietnam Peace Parade Committee, 11" h. x 8.5" w., 1971, scarce, $45-85.

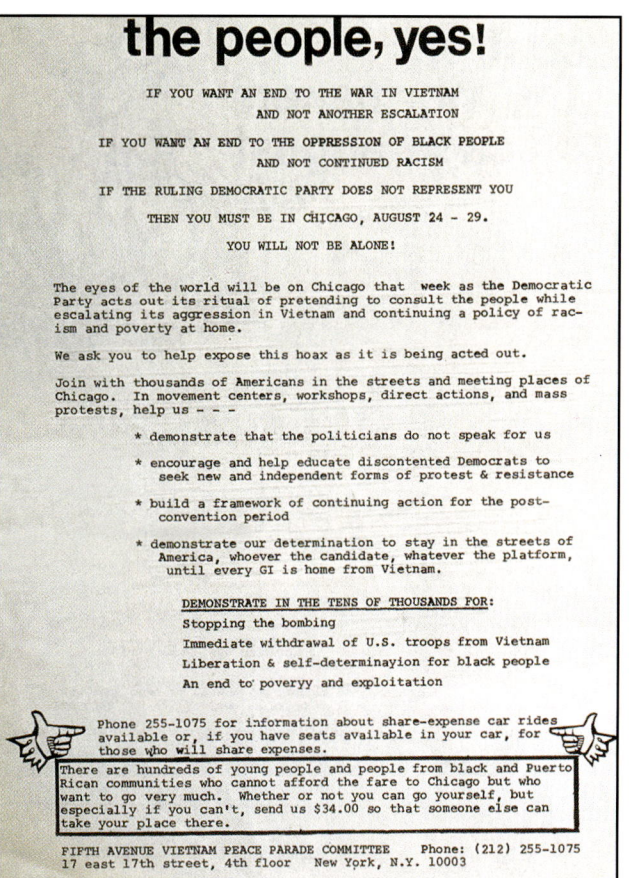

Reverse side of handbill says "the people, yes!" and outlines additional information regarding the demonstration.

The Feminine Mystique, written by Betty Freidan, was a driving force behind the 1960s "Women's Lib" movement. In 1966, Friedan co-founded NOW (National Organization for Women), and became its first president. Feminist author Gloria Steinem also became a prominent figure in the movement. NOW was the primary advocate of the ERA (Equal Rights Amendment).

Tinted photographic poster, entitled "Woman's Lib, Stand Up For Equal Rights," shows a woman standing with men at urinal, copyright Creative Posters, Los Angeles, CA, 7" h. x 9" w., 1969, scarce, $45-85.

Poster, "New England Congress to Unite Women," N.E. Women's Coalition, Boston, MA, 22" h. x 14" w., 1971, scarce, $50-100.

Black light poster, "American Woman #280," artist Rick Ambrose, The Third Eye Inc., New York, 34" h. x 21" w., 1970, scarce, $50-125.

Migrant farm workers were organized by Cesar Chavez and the United Farm Workers of the AFL-CIO. The May 1969 Boycott Poster "Don't Eat Grapes" includes a quote at the bottom by Chavez from a letter to the United Farm Workers, AFL-CIO, Delano, California: *"We are men and women who have suffered and endured much and not only because of our abject poverty but because we have been kept poor. The colors of our skins, the languages of our cultural and native origins, the lack of formal education, the exclusion from the democratic process, the numbers of our slain in recent wars—all these burdens generation after generation have sought to demoralize us, to break our human spirit. But God knows that we are not beasts of burden, we are not agricultural implements or rented slaves, we are men. We are men locked in a death struggle against man's inhumanity to man."*

Poster, "Don't Eat Grapes," International Grape Boycott Day, May 10, 1969, artist Milton Glazer, 36" h. x 24" w., 1969, uncommon, $35-65; A warehouse find of these posters several years ago has increased availability.

Until 1965, the activities of the SDS were mainly limited to civil rights causes, but later they became involved with ending the war in Vietnam. The SDS often formed alliances with the Black Panthers and other radical groups to engage more protesters. An extreme terrorist faction known as the Weathermen (Weather Underground, originally called the Revolutionary Youth Movement I) separated from the SDS in 1969 and began to carry out violent revolutionary acts of terrorism to achieve their goals, ultimately being implicated in a number of federal building and campus bombings. Their symbol was the "fork salute," four fingers in the air to show camaraderie with Charles Manson who killed actress Sharon Tate and plunged a fork into her stomach.[5]

Newsletter, *Student Peace Union Bulletin*, from a student organization that preceded and influenced the hippie peace movement, 1962, scarce, $35-65.

Students for a Democratic Society (SDS) newspaper, *SDS New Left Notes*, v5 n1, June 30, 1969, 8 pages, Boston, MA, 16.5" h. x 11.5" w., uncommon, $25-45.

The Port Huron Statement, the proclamation of the Students for a Democratic Society (SDS), had as a lead writer Tom Hayden, former editor of the student newspaper at the University of Michigan. It proposed that students initiate reform within society, a role previously led by organized labor, and called for students to join in a movement to establish "participatory democracy."[6] It opens: *"We are the people of this generation, bred in at least modest comfort, looking uncomfortably to the world we inherit."*

"The Port Huron Statement," an early copy of the manifesto that was originally mimeographed and distributed to college campuses, printed by the SDS, 11" h. x 8.5" w., 1963, very rare, $150-300.

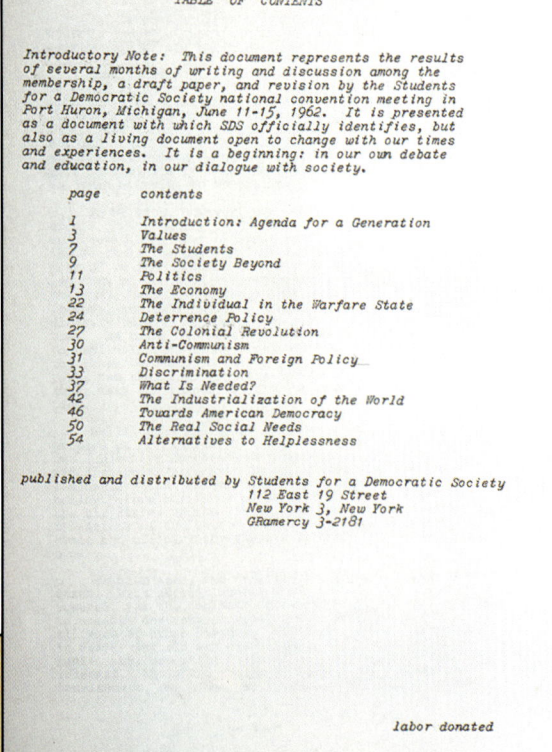

Table of contents and purpose for the creation of "The Port Huron Statement."

Billy Jack movie theater window card, a cult favorite portraying the hippie's "everyman hero," played by Tom McLaughlin, whose character portrays a half breed American Indian, former special forces Viet Nam vet pacifist, who defends hippie causes in the Southwest, Warner Bros. Inc., 36" h. x 14" w., 1973, scarce, $50-100.

Poster, "Join the SMC" (Student Mobilization Committee), announcing a Student Strike Nov. 3rd to protest the war, 17" h. x 11" w., 1969, rare, $100-250.

Concurrent with the growth of the SDS was the development of the Free Speech Movement. An area of Telegraph Avenue called the Bancroft Strip, adjacent to the University of California at Berkeley, had been a place where students would give speeches, distribute pamphlets, sign petitions, and enlist people in their causes. The Berkeley Free Speech Movement, led by junior philosophy major Mario Savio, started with a sit-in protest in support of five students who were brought up on disciplinary action for expressing their political rights in September 1965. The sit-in resulted in the eventual arrest of 500 students at Sproul Hall on the Berkeley campus. The police moved in to break up the protest, but the ensuing demonstrations eventually forced the campus to close, resulting in national news headlines. The Free Speech Movement at the University of California at Berkeley campus is considered the first major confrontation of the 1960's student revolution.

Free Speech Movement (FSM), *Sounds & Songs of the Demonstration*, 33 1/3 LP album, Cireco Music, San Francisco, 1965, scarce, $50-100.

From top: enamel and rhinestone vote pin, common, $10-25; plastic VOTE pendant, 3" dia., common, $10-25; polyester scarf, uncommon, $15-35. Apparel accessories were commonly designed to be worn to remind people to go to the polls and vote, a popular cause enthusiastically endorsed by hippies to "dethrone" Nixon in the 1972 presidential race that ultimately failed. *Collection courtesy of Gary Moise, 70's-store.com at Orange Trading Company, Orange, MA*

Back: 33 1/3 LP album, *Wake Up America, Abbie Hoffman Sings On His Friends*, Big Toe Records, 1968, scarce, $35-65. *Left to right:* Woman's Lib box, Franco-American Novelty Co., New York, 1972 uncommon, $10-25; "Woman's Rights Now" pin, 1970, common, $5-15; Spiro Agnew novelty mouthwash, Made In USA Co., L.A., CA, 1970, uncommon, $10-20; Spiro Agnew glass ashtray, uncommon, $15-35; milk glass bottle with transfer of protesting flower child, 9" h., (post hippie period), uncommon, $15-35.

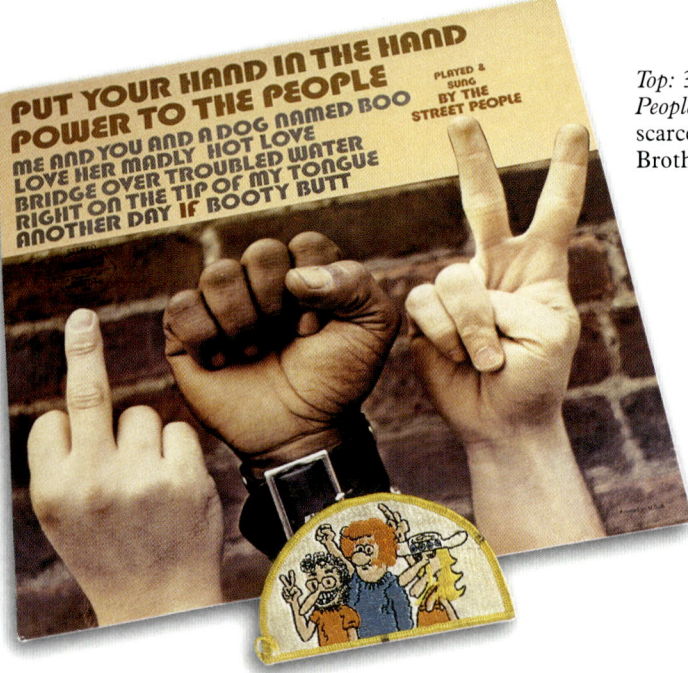

Top: 33 1/3 LP album *Put Your Hand In The Hand, Power to the People*, Pickwick Records, sung by The Street People, 1969, scarce, $35-65. *Bottom:* cloth patch of the Fabulous Furry Freak Brothers, a Gilbert Shelton creation, 1968, rare, $45-85.

Top: armband "Stop the Killing," 1967, uncommon, $15-35. *Top left:* metal pinback symbol of bi-racial peace effort, Vietnam Peace Parade Committee of New York for April 27, 1968 protest march, 2 1/3" dia., scarce, $25-50. A celluloid version (not shown) is more common, $10-25. *Bottom left:* "Billy Jack for President" metal photo pinback, 1972, rare, $35-65. *Right:* post card to gain support for an antiwar rally on Oct. 13, uncommon, $10-25. *Collection courtesy of Gary Moise, 70's-store.com at Orange Trading Company, Orange, MA.*

Edward Abbey, an environmental activist, drew attention to the harm done to national forests and parks by big business and government. Many of his followers, drop-outs seeking a simpler, more peaceful lifestyle of solitude in the rural areas, were considered the first environmental activists. Among them, was the environmental group, Earth First!

Belly Buttons, 3" pinback and Stitch Its cloth patch, both on mailing postcard, Kaymac Distribution Systems, Royal Oak, MI, 1970, promoting environmental awareness, uncommon, $10-25 each.

Top from left: three ring binder with hippie slogans that were popularized by the television show *Rowan and Martin's Laugh-In*, 1968, uncommon, $15-35; high school yearbook with antiwar and protest slogans, 1970, uncommon, $10-25. *Bottom from left: The Realist* magazine, Nov.-Dec., 1969, common, $5-10; paper placemat, Save Our Environment c. 1971, uncommon, $5-10.

The group known as the Chicago 7 consisted of seven young men arrested and tried as leaders of the antiwar protests at the Democratic National Convention in 1968. These young men were Rennie Davis, David Dellinger, John Froines, Tom Hayden, Abbie Hoffman, Jerry Rubin, and Lee Weiner. Bobby Seale, a Black Panther leader, was also involved.

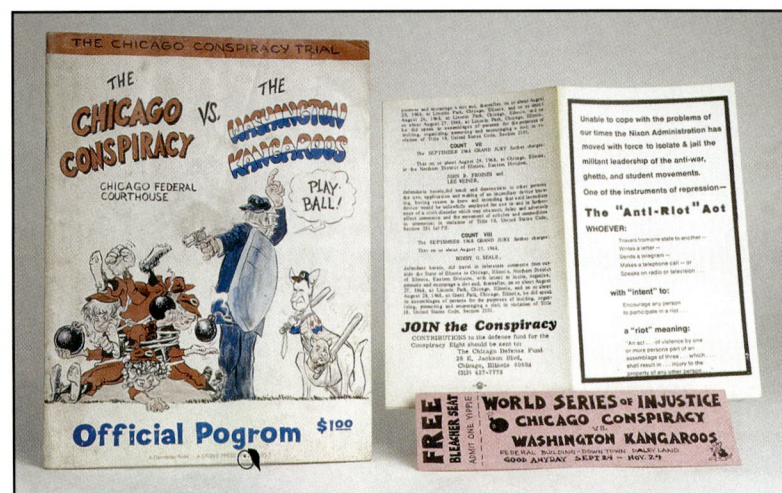

Newspaper insert poster announcing a rally to join the conspiracy at the Park St. subway stop on the Boston Commons, scarce, $25-45.

From left: satirical program of the Chicago 7 trial printed to resemble a baseball game program, Chicago Conspirators vs. Washington Establishment, scarce, $65-125; brochure, "Anti-Riot Act," describing the Nixon administrations repressive program against militant groups and requesting citizens support their cause by joining, scarce, $45-85. Ticket satirizing the trial of the Chicago 7, scarce, $35-65.

Antiwar protest stickers, 1968, 3" by 5", common, $5-10 each.

Top from left: package of 6 match books with a variety of peace symbols, printed by Houston Black Light and Poster Co., c. 1967, uncommon, $10-25; Missing in action (MIA) metal bracelet with impressed name of U.S. soldier, worn to show support for those missing in action, uncommon, $15-35. *Bottom from left:* MIA book of matches with photo of missing soldier, uncommon, $10-25; pinbacks for two different antiwar protest marches on Washington, 1969, common, $5-15; butane lighter with popular rally slogan, "war is not healthy", 1967, common, $10-20.

The popularization of chants such as "power to the people" used by student protesters, civil rights advocates and other causes spawned the Protest Button industry. This industry produced thousands of varieties of "power" and "cause" pins sold in head shops and underground boutiques. One popular store was Underground Uplift Unlimited (U.U.U.) that sold buttons, stickers, and posters for as little as twenty-five cents each. Located at 28 St. Mark's Place, New York City in the East Village across from the Electric Circus and near the Fillmore East concert hall, the store always had hundreds of different protest and antiwar pins in stock. Other pin manufacturers were:

Vagabond, West Carrollton, Ohio
Wendell's, Minneapolis, Minnesota
Fargo Rubber Stamp Company, Fargo, North Dakota
Big Store, McDougal Street, New York City
Hip Products, Chicago, Illinois
NG Slater Corp., New York City
Sandyval, Bleecker St. in Greenwich Village, New York City
Marvic, Brooklyn New York
Be-in Buttons, Houston, Texas
Big Little Store, Polk Street, San Francisco, California
Wicker, Berkeley, California
Horn Company, Philadelphia, Pennsylvania

Top from left: butane lighter, "reach out for your brother" promoting solidarity between whites and blacks, 1967, common, $10-20; leather choker with metal symbol of an "ankh" which represents life, common, $10-20; "Batman Loves Robin" pin, satirical statement on the Gay Rights Movement, scarce, $25-45. All remaining pins promote the environmental cause "Save the Earth", uncommon, $10-25.

A variety of popular pinbacks promoting various causes and rallies of the late 1960s, most are common or uncommon, $10-50.

There was no official end to the marches and rallies in which hippies took part, however, much of the active protest diminished shortly after the signing of a cease fire agreement on January 23, 1973. The result of the cease-fire agreement was gradual American troop withdrawal from Vietnam.

FUGS T-shirt, the popular singing protest group included Ed Saunders and Tuli Kupferberg, New York City, 1967, rare, $50-100.

Poster, "Keep the Faith Baby," a saying popularized by Reverend Adam Clayton Powell, the Harlem Congressman who championed minority rights, printed by Pandora Productions, 1967, uncommon, $35-65.

By many accounts, the gay liberation movement began Friday envening, June 27, 1969, after the police raided a Sheridan Square gay bar in Greenwich Village, New York. This raid sparked what is now known as the Stonewall Riots. The Gay Activists Alliance originated at Ohio State University in the 1970s and used a Big Lambda as a symbol for the Gay and Lesbian Rights Movement.

From top: anti Viet Nam war and anti draft pins, 1968, uncommon, $15-35; pinbacks supporting Gay Rights and Woman's Lib, scarce, 1970, $35-65.

WNCR, 99.5 was the first radio station to play underground, progressive music in Cleveland. This station, with disc jockeys that used their first names, played 50 minutes of non-stop, commercial free music. The poster shown here has a nice photo of a hippie wearing an American flag hat next to an unusual peace sign flag. The station was eventually surpassed by WMMS which then became mainstream, putting WNCR out of business.

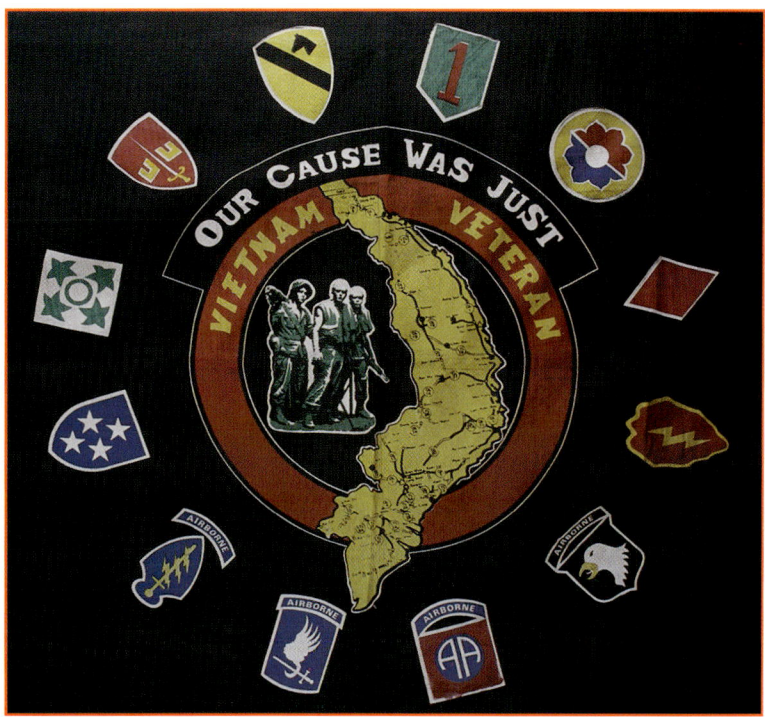

Cloth banner "Our Cause Was Just," sentiment about how the futility of the war affected the way Americans viewed returning soldiers who often felt a need to defend their actions, 30" h. x 56" w., uncommon (post hippie period), $15-35.

WNCR 99.5 Stereo poster, Join The Renaissance," 28" h. x 20" w., c. 1969, scarce, $50-100. *Photograph courtesy of Walter "Hawkeye" Potaznick, West Bridgewater, MA.*

Hand painted round cork board Viet Nam souvenir brought home by U.S. soldiers, 12" dia., 1969, uncommon, $15-35.

Chapter Three
Jus' Folks: Hand Made Relics

Hippie folk art was quite colorful, often using innovative materials with an emphasis on recycled components and an untrained approach to composition. In many instances, hippie folk art was reminiscent of today's popular outsider art. Remnants of old clothes, patches, safety pins, paper clips, chewing gum and cigarette wrappers, and day-glo paints were all used.

The folk painted suede cowboy hat, suitcase, and wood guitar shown here are all intricately decorated and probably took several months to complete. The details in the drawings often reveal the personal experiences of the owner through symbols and events common to that time period.

Hand painted suede western hat, very detailed, involving several months of work by an enthusiastic artist showing hippie images and slogans, very rare, $200-400.

Side view of hand painted folk hat

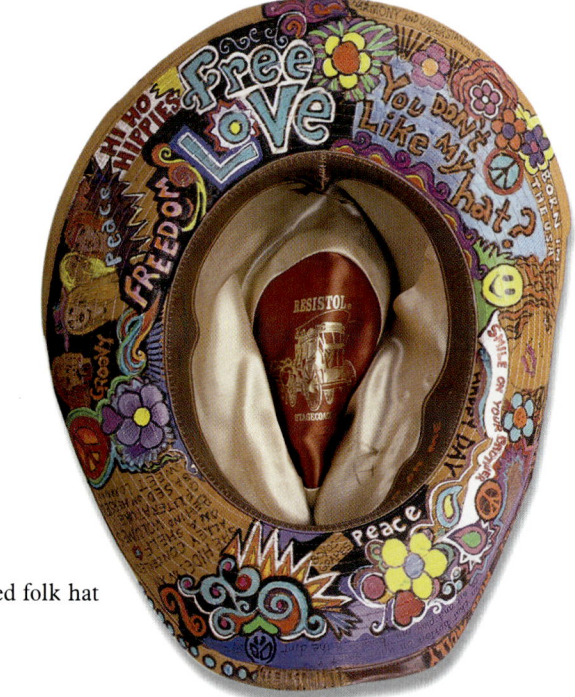

View of underside of hand painted folk hat

Hand painted wooden carry case with peace symbols, guitar and clock, 1966, rare, $75-150.

Hand painted guitar with peace, love, rainbow and smiling sun painted in psychedelic style, rare, $150-300.

Back side of hand painted guitar with peace and other hippie symbols.

This interesting old hat was handmade by some enterprising hippie who probably made them to sell at street fairs. This risky fashion was created at a time when aluminum beer cans had a removable pull tab. Vests and dresses were also popular subjects for this form of hippie folk art. This particular example is embellished with gaudy, plastic pink carnations.

Hat made from aluminum can pull tab tops. In the late 1960's, the aluminum beer can tabs were pulled entirely off the top of the can. Later this was changed for safety reasons with the top pushed in but remaining connected to the can. Hippies found a utilitarian use for the discarded pull tabs by making hats and vests from them. These were then sold at street fairs, very rare, $75-150.

Following the assassination of Dr. Martin Luther King Jr. in April of 1968, this flag was used at a demonstration in Washington, D.C. It was also used as a curtain in a college fraternity house during the early 1970s. The flag was made from cotton blend bed sheets that were hand cut, stitched, and dyed.

Beaded suede bag, quite popular with hippies, this one especially unusual with symbols for male and female, an intricate geometric starburst pattern, and 5 different bead colors, scarce, $50-100. Single bead color bags (not shown) without design are quite common, $10-25.

Peace sign rally flag, hand cut, sewn and dyed from bed sheets by college students. This one was used in the November 15, 1969 March on Washington, rare, $75-150.

"Flying Eyeball" embroidered western shirt with Von Dutch flying eyeball design, a graphic image used in rock concert posters and LSD related items, 1972, uncommon, $25-50.

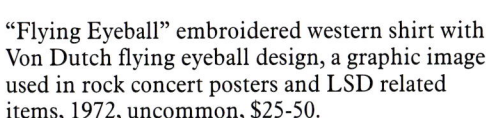

From left: leather wine pouch often carried by hippies, common, $10-25. *Courtesy of Gary Moise, 70's-store.com at Orange Trading Company, Orange, MA;* unusual leather hippie hat with hand cut diamonds and hearts, scarce, $75-125.

Overcoat with numerous hand painted peace symbols worn at antiwar rallies, c. 1967, scarce, $75-150.

Hand sewn shirt made from fifty pound flour sacks, many of these shirts were made in Mexico, cotton, uncommon, $10-25.

An American flag 70" high by 93" wide that is identical in appearance to the top armband in this photo, was used on stage at the August 1969 Woodstock Music Festival. It was found in a barn, and brought $22,705 at an auction at Sotheby's in New York City on May 23, 2002.[7]

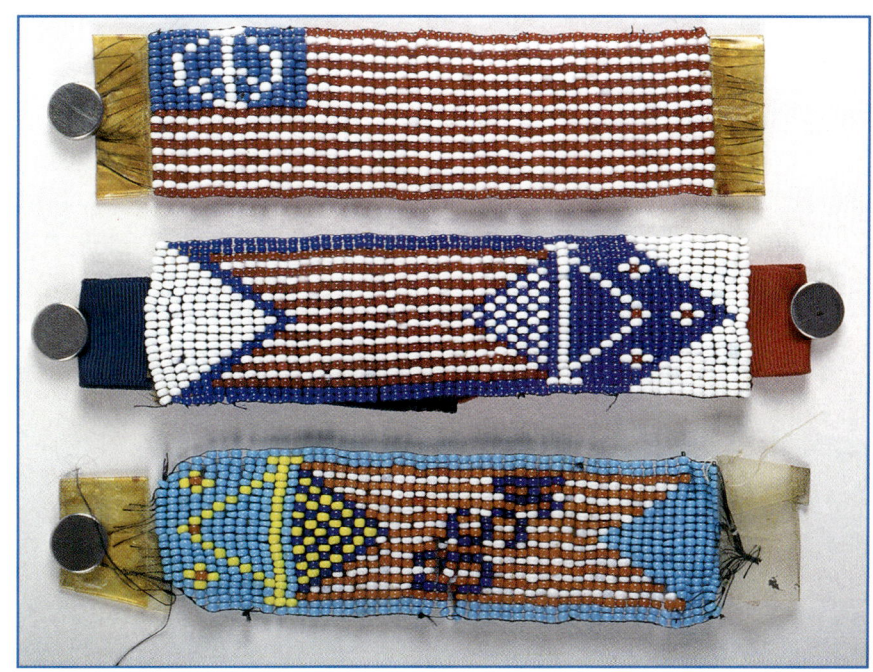

Hand made beaded arm bands worn during antiwar marches, scarce, $50-100.

From left: tassel belt handmade from cut, multi-colored, circular pieces of suede attached by round metal clips, c. 1967, scarce, $35-65; round suede purse whip stitched using multi-color leather pieces in a pie shape, scarce, $50-100.

Commune at night, hippie family reading in their tent, oil on board, 16" h. x 20" w., 1970, rare, $50-150.

The Head, color pencil drawing, 24" h. x 16" w., 1970, rare, $100-200.

Grok, a word used by hippies that meant "to absorb, imbibe, embody sensations or information[8]", oil on board painting, 16" h. x 20" w., 1972, rare, $100-200.

Hippie couple with sunglasses giving peace sign, oil on canvas, abstract-cubist style, 24" h. x 18" w., c. 1967, rare, $150-300.

Color lithograph, artist John L. Eastman, signed in pencil, 22" h. x 16" w., c. 1967, rare, $150-300.

Iridescent watercolor on paper, psychedelic cowboy, 30" h. x 24" w., c. 1968, rare, $100-200.

Painting, psychedelic super heroes, acrylic on masonite, 36" h. x 34" w., 1972, rare, $150-300.

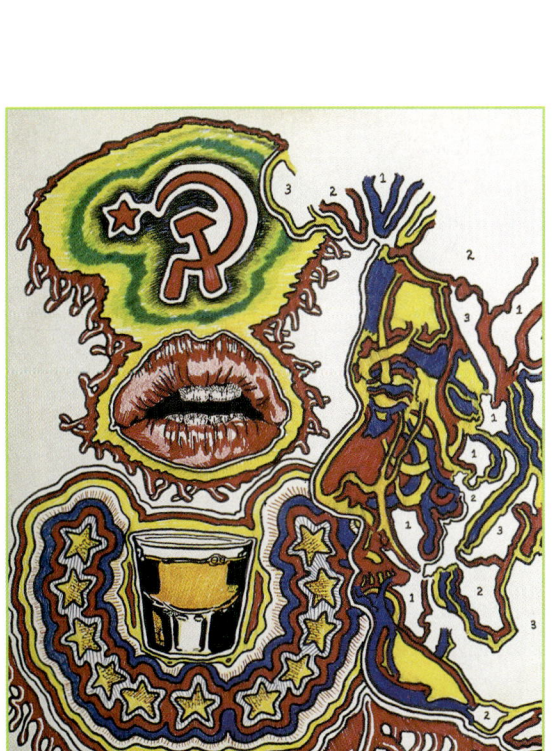

Psychedelic op art illustration of hammer and sickle, glass of water, mouth and facial profile, color pencil on paper, 15" h. x 12" w., 1972, scarce, $50-100.

Oil painting on masonite, hippies hitchhiking to San Francisco, 10" h. x 22" w., rare, c. 1967, *Courtesy of Gary Moise, 70's-store.com at Orange Trading Company, Orange, MA.* $100-200.

Oil on masonite, titled "Crepusculo,", four skeletons carrying a casket, 12" h. x 16" w., scarce, 1970, $50-150.

Acid trip collage, mixed media on masonite, references to pot and LSD, 30" h. x 24" w., c. 1967, rare. *Courtesy of Gary Moise, 70's-store.com at Orange Trading Company, Orange, MA.* $100-200

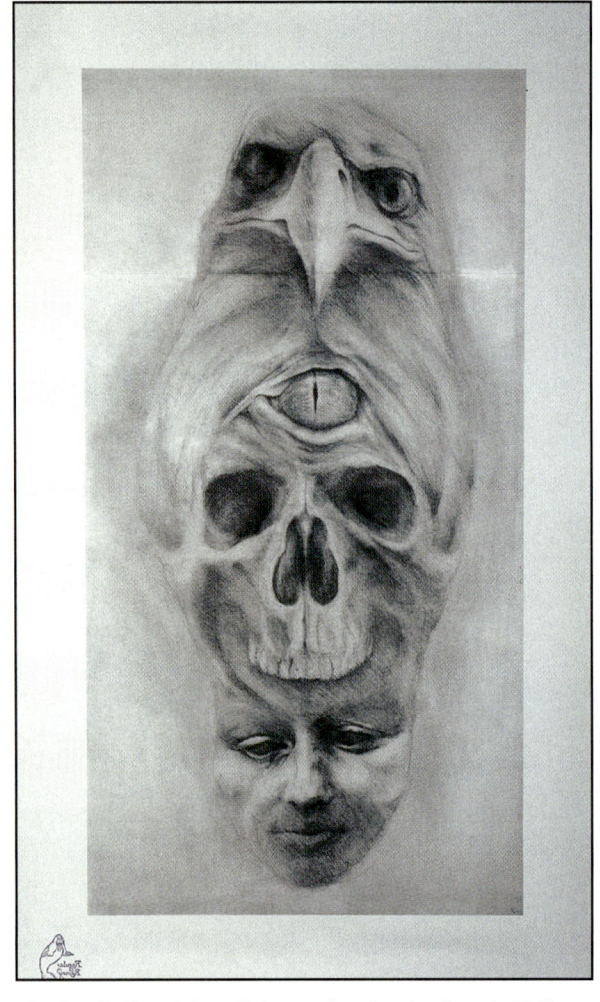

Eagle, skull and face, lithograph print, by Regula Zeller Rainey. Rainey was born in Basel, Switzerland, studied at the Art Institute of Chicago in the early 1960's, and received a M.F.A. from the University of Chicago. She was involved in theatrical and multi-media design for the Electric Light Theater before passing away in 1995 at the age of 54. 32" h. x 24" w., c. 1967, scarce, $35-65.

Painting, oil on canvas, Kent State, after a magazine cover, 24" h. x 18" w., 1970, scarce. *Courtesy of Gary Moise, 70's-store.com at Orange Trading Company, Orange, MA.* $50-150.

Spin art, paper placed on spindle, as it spun paint was dropped onto it making a psychedelic pattern, 8" h. x 12" w., 1965, common, $25-45.

From top: embossed copper sheet on wood with finger peace sign, 8" h. x 8" w., 1970, uncommon, $25-50; 60s symbols, oil on canvas, 12" h. x 18" w., c. 1968, uncommon, $35-65.

Handmade necklace of copper wire and brass, c. 1966, scarce, $50-100.

From top: hair barrette, metal and turquoise beads, 4" h. x 8" w., uncommon, $15-35; rawhide and wood bead necklace with polished abalone shell pendant, scarce, $45-85; rawhide necklace with hammered pendant made from blacksmith nails, stamped with artist logo, scarce, $45-85.

Youth hostels in Europe were hosts to many American hippies. During the summer of 1969, a rumor spread quickly throughout these hostels about a cache of trade beads that was unearthed in an area of Africa called either Bhooleman or Ghooleman, and brought to Amsterdam. In fact, several stores near the red light district were selling dirt covered beads from large wooden bins. Years later the truth about the beads became evident—they were colorful glass beads actually made in Murano, Italy.

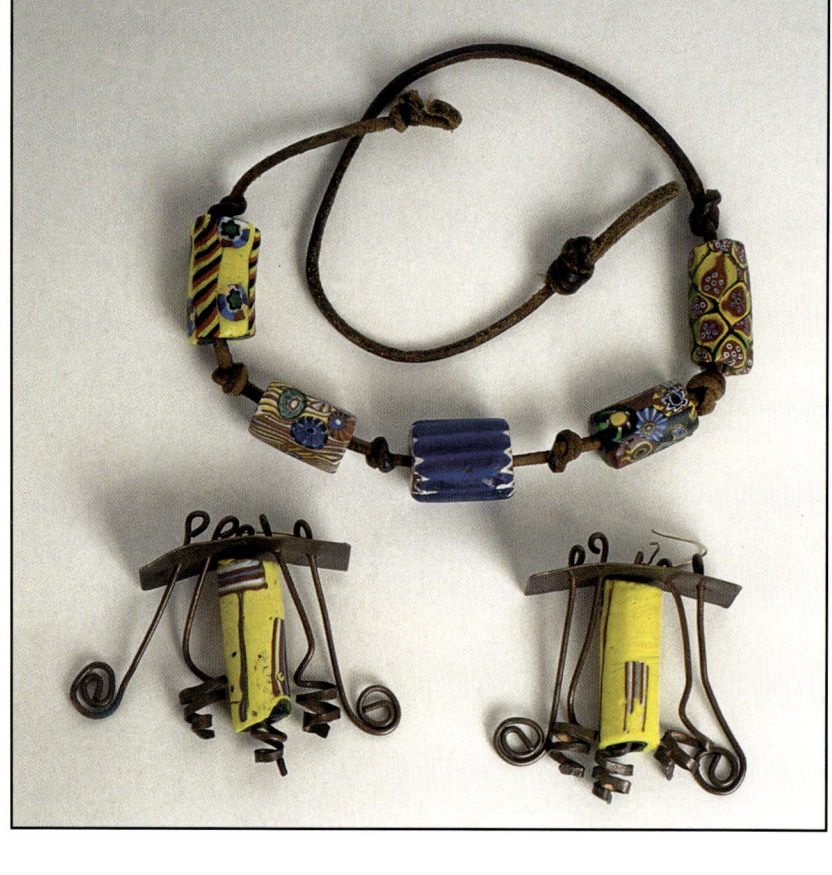

From top: rawhide necklace with Murano glass beads, c. 1969, scarce, $50-100; value varies with number and color of beads. Murano glass bead and copper wire earrings, scarce, $35-65.

From top: rawhide and wood beaded necklace, pendant fashioned from sliced tree branch with flower power painted design, common, $10-25; hammered brass necklace, uncommon, $35-65.

From top: hammered aluminum pin, abstract floral design, uncommon, $10-25; necklace and pendant made from paper clips and chewing gum wrappers, scarce, $35-65.

From top: brass safety pin and bead bracelet, rare, $35-65; black safety pin and bead necklace, rare, $45-85.

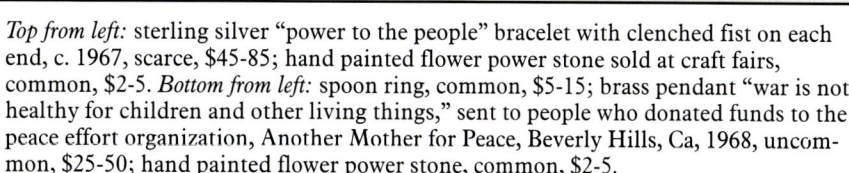

Top from left: sterling silver "power to the people" bracelet with clenched fist on each end, c. 1967, scarce, $45-85; hand painted flower power stone sold at craft fairs, common, $2-5. *Bottom from left:* spoon ring, common, $5-15; brass pendant "war is not healthy for children and other living things," sent to people who donated funds to the peace effort organization, Another Mother for Peace, Beverly Hills, Ca, 1968, uncommon, $25-50; hand painted flower power stone, common, $2-5.

Center photo: *From top:* leather embossed, painted pendant and necklace with Native American Indian motif, c. 1967, common, $10-25; rawhide and wood bead necklace with hammered pendant made from blacksmith nails, uncommon, $15-35; glass and white metal collage pendant with embedded flower, common, $10-25.

From top: painted leather strip bracelet, common, $10-25; bead and leather necklace, peace symbol motif, scarce, $45-85.

From left: beaded necklace, scarce, $45-85; Alpaca wool bag, made in Mexico, uncommon, $15-35. Alpaca wool vests (not shown) with similar design were also popular during this period. *Courtesy of Gary Moise, 70's-store.com at Orange Trading Company, Orange, MA.*

Chalk statue entitled "The Wedding," made by Paula's Inc., St. Paul, MN, 1974, 14" h. x 10" w. Back of groom's shirt says "marijuana pickers union #13," very rare, $75-150.

Handmade wool knit afghan with embroidered protest slogans, 1968, rare, $75-150.

Left: black velvet art marijuana leaf painting "Yerba Buena High" (Spanish for *good grass*), 16" h. x 12.5" w., uncommon, $15-35; lucite coasters with embedded marijuana leaf, 5" square, c. 1966, scarce, $20-45. *Right:* leather document bag with hand tooled marijuana leaf design, 12" h. x 8" w., 2" deep, scarce, $45-85; hand made pottery vase with Flow Blue marijuana leaf design for indoor growing, 4" h. x 5" w., scarce, $25-50.

From left: patchwork suede purse, uncommon, $25-45; leather link purse, common, $10-25. *Courtesy of Gary Moise, 70's-store.com at Orange Trading Company, Orange, MA.*

Hand painted plastic sheet on wood base entitled "Which one is God's favorite child?", peace sign design used in head of children, New American Gallery, 1432 Main St, Cincinnati, OH 45210, phone 621-7445, 10" h. x 8" w., rare, $100-250.

From left: purse made from old denim blue jeans, common, $5-15; cotton purse, peace sign, peace doves, and make love not war motif, scarce, $25-50. *Background:* unused vintage textile fabric similar to purse. Hippie graphics yardage can vary from a low of $2 to over $75 per yard depending upon the design, designer, and amount available. This antiwar design would likely fall in the $10-20 per yard range.

From left: ceramic peace sign vase, 10" h. x 9" w., scarce, $45-85; Peter Max glass ashtray, 5" square, uncommon, $35-65; pottery vase, 14" h. x 6" w., 1965, scarce, $35-65.

Cut and welded, orange painted, sheet metal lawn ornament, LOVE with dove, 28" h. x 6" w., rare, $100-250; green Smiley Face flower sheet metal window ornament, rare, $50-150. *Courtesy of Gary Moise, The 70's-store.com at Orange Trading Company, Orange, MA.*

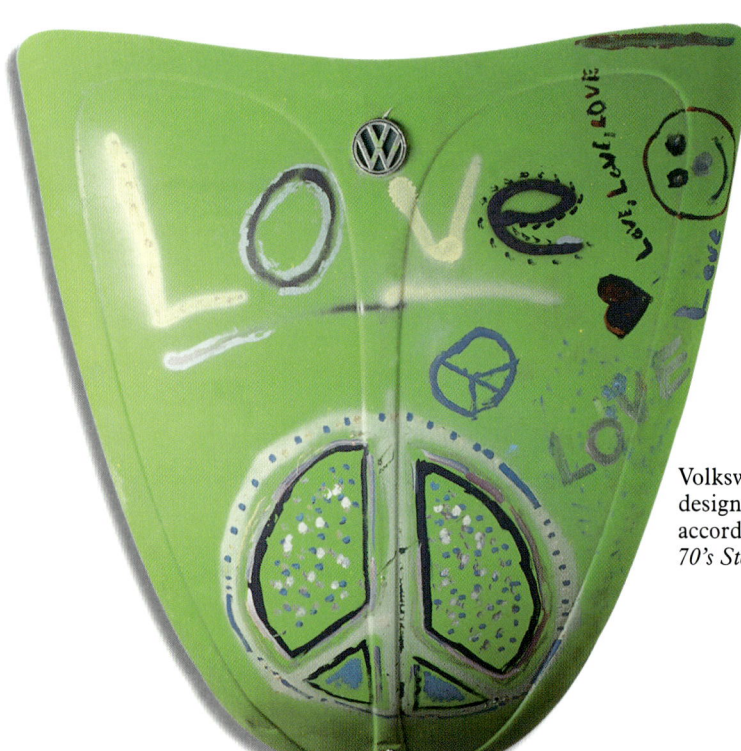

Volkswagen Beetle front hood with hand painted hippie design, c. 1966, scarce, $50-150, price will vary greatly according to quality of the artistry. *Courtesy of Gary Moise, The 70's Store at Orange Trading Company, Orange, MA.*

From left: leaded stained glass mountain sunset with marijuana leaf design, 14" h. x 10" w., rare, $150-300; painted wood smiling sun, 14" dia., scarce, $45-85. *Courtesy of Gary Moise, The 70's Store at Orange Trading Company, Orange, MA.*

From left: pottery candleholder with incised flower power design, 8" h. x 5" w., scarce, $45-85; pottery vase with zig-zag and other unusual incised designs, 7" h. x 5" w., rare, $65-125. Pottery pieces similar to these were produced at craft studios like the Penland School of Crafts in the mountains of North Carolina. *Courtesy of Gary Moise, The 70's Store at Orange Trading Company, Orange, MA;* multi-media hand formed clay figure with multiple head silhouette and painted flag design on iron base, 10" h. x 7" w., 1965, rare, $200-350.

Reverse side of multi-media clay figure with multiple head silhouette and painted flag design.

Lithograph print of commune hippies celebrating under a rainbow next to their flower power peace bus, artist T. Carpenter, 18" h. x 12" w., c. 1968, rare, $50-100.

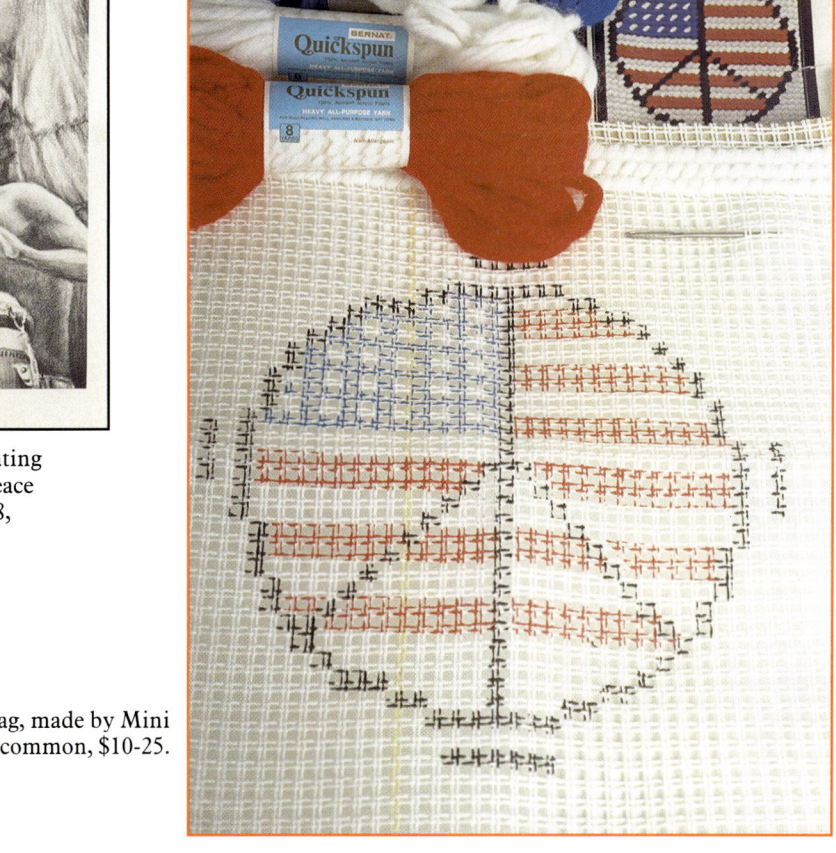

Needlework peace sign flag, made by Mini Quickpoint, 1968, uncommon, $10-25.

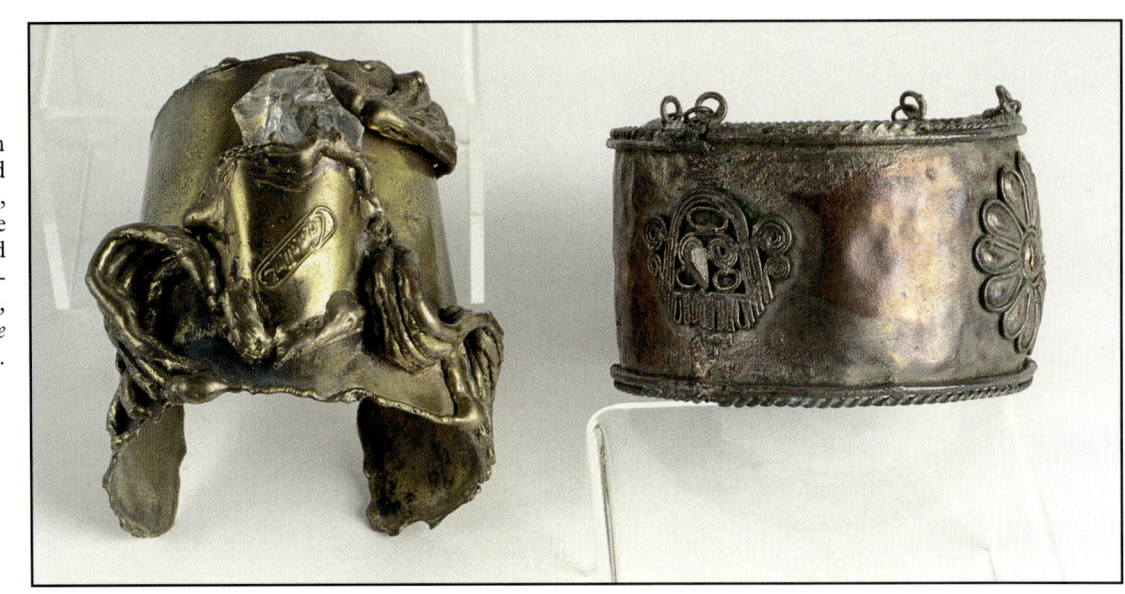

From left: brass bracelet with applied design of hammered frog and glass crystal, scarce, $50-100; Middle Eastern style silver bracelet with applied floral design, uncommon, $35-65. *Courtesy of Gary Moise, 70's-store.com at Orange Trading Company, Orange, MA.*

Bronze ankh with arms candle stand, signed MMA, 9" h. x 4" w., 1970, rare, $50-100. *Photograph courtesy of Walter "Hawkeye" Potaznick, West Bridgewater, MA.*

Hippie painting, oil on canvas, signed Robbins, 16" h. x 12" w., c. 1968, scarce, $75-150. *Photograph courtesy of Walter "Hawkeye" Potaznick, West Bridgewater, MA.*

In God We Trust, oil on canvas, signed J. D. Handy Jr., 40" h. x 30" w., c. 1966, rare, $200-400. *Photograph courtesy of Walter "Hawkeye" Potaznick, West Bridgewater, MA.*

Biker hippies, oil on board, signed Dona, 16" h. x 20" w., 1972, rare, $100-300. *Photograph courtesy of Walter "Hawkeye" Potaznick, West Bridgewater, MA.*

Two hippies, colored pencil on paper, signed Dashcam, 1967, 16" h. x 20" w., 1972, rare, $75-150. *Photograph courtesy of Walter "Hawkeye" Potaznick, West Bridgewater, MA.*

Hippie, oil on wood, signed L.V., 16" h. x 8" w., 1973, scarce, $50-100. *Photograph courtesy of Walter "Hawkeye" Potaznick, West Bridgewater, MA.*

Left: Man in the Moon pottery vase with incised hand peace sign design, 12" high, 7" wide, signed PM on one side and RG on the other, c. 1969, rare, $75-$150. *Photograph courtesy of Walter "Hawkeye" Potaznick, West Bridgewater, MA.*

Right: Rear view of Man in the Moon pottery vase showing peace sign and applied marijuana leaf design.

Oil on canvas titled "Love," signed Joe Kantor, listed in *Who's Who in American Art*, 36" high, 30" wide, c. 1967, rare, $150-$350. *Photograph courtesy of Walter "Hawkeye" Potaznick, West Bridgewater, MA.*

Chapter Four
Feeling Groovy: The Drug Culture*

The 1960s gave birth to the pervasive use of illegal drugs, mainly hallucinogenics such as LSD (lysergic acid diethylamide), mescaline, and marijuana. Prior to this period, marijuana was used primarily by poets, artists and musicians to enhance their art. LSD, a mind-altering chemical that was legal until 1966, was virtually unknown to American society in the early sixties. It became popular through the publicity given to the "acid guru," Timothy Leary. Leary was a psychology professor at Harvard when he began experimenting with LSD in 1960. He started the "League of Spiritual Discovery," an LSD advocacy group, and during this period he coined the phrase "turn on, tune in, drop out." This meant look at what was happening around you, drop out of school, and search for true meaning in life. He was supported in his efforts by a former colleague from Harvard, Richard Alpert, who later became Baba Ram Dass after spending a year in an Indian ashram.

*The material in this chapter is presented for its historical contribution to the hippie period. The author neither advocates nor condones the recreational use of any illicit pharmaceutical substances.

Board game, "Scam, the Game of International Dope Smuggling," 1971, copyright Brown Bag Enterprises, 20" long, 10" w., very rare, $200-350.

Anti-drug poster with psychedelic black light graphics, "Will they turn you on or will they turn on you," designed by WB, printed by the U.S. Department of Health, Education and Welfare, National Institute of Mental Health, 28" h. x 22" w., very rare, $250-400.

Playing board for "Scam, the Game of International Dope Smuggling."

Drug related pinbacks vary from $10-65 depending on slogan, graphics and scarcity. *Top from left:* "God is Alive in a Sugar Cube" pinback, uncommon, $10-25; "The Chemicals are Coming" pinback, scarce, $20-45. *Bottom from left:* "Smoke Grass" pinback, scarce, $15-35; "Pyschedelicize Suburbia" pinback, uncommon, $10-25.

Period drug related items are relatively scarce and in high demand. *Rear:* silk scarf, Mexican flag and marijuana leaf motif, uncommon, $25-45. *Front from left:* brass bird hash pipe, scarce, $45-85. *Courtesy of Gary Moise, 70's-store.com, located at Orange Trading Co., Orange, MA.* Instructional journal, *How to Roll a Joint*, 24 pages, copyright Joint Projects, Los Angeles, CA, 11" h. x 8" w., 1971, rare, $50-100.

Metal, Impeach Nixon roach clip, made by American Horse Ent., Fulsom, Nixon wearing headphones being flushed down Watergate toilet, 3.5" h. c. 1973, scarce, $50-100.

Timothy Leary wristwatch, 12 O'Clock High Inc., numbers replaced with names of popular illicit drugs of the period, 1970, very rare, $200-350.

"Timothy Leary's Holding Together," flyer to solicit funds for the legal defense to earn Timothy Leary's freedom. In 1970, Leary was serving a ten year sentence for marijuana possession when the radical Weather Underground helped him escape from a San Luis Obispo, California jail. He was apprehended in Afghanistan three years later. This flyer was printed just prior to his escape, 15" high, 10" wide, 1970, very rare, $200-$400.

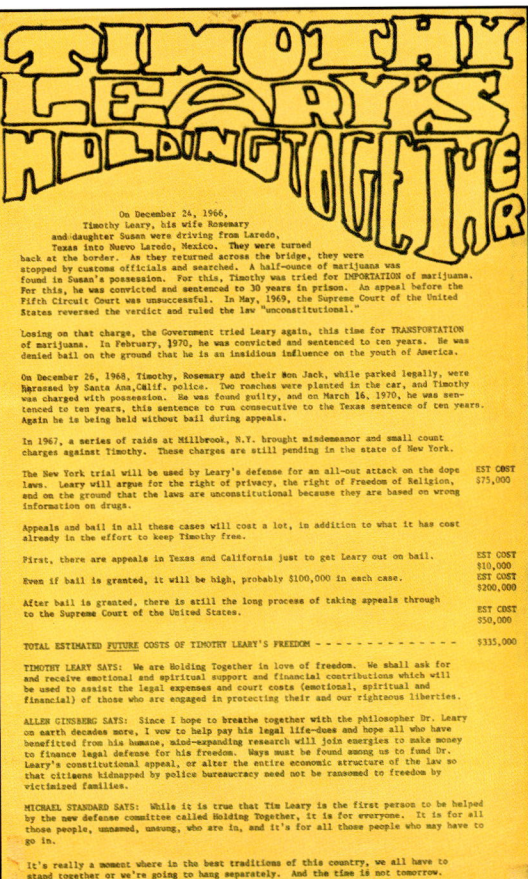

From left: 3 piece metal stash can with flower power design, removable internal sifter, base with paper label, made by Stash Can Enterprises, Oakland, CA, 4" dia., rare, $50-100; plastic stash box with drug store design, prices of commonly used recreational drugs of the late 1960's, 6" h. x 4" w., scarce, $35-65.

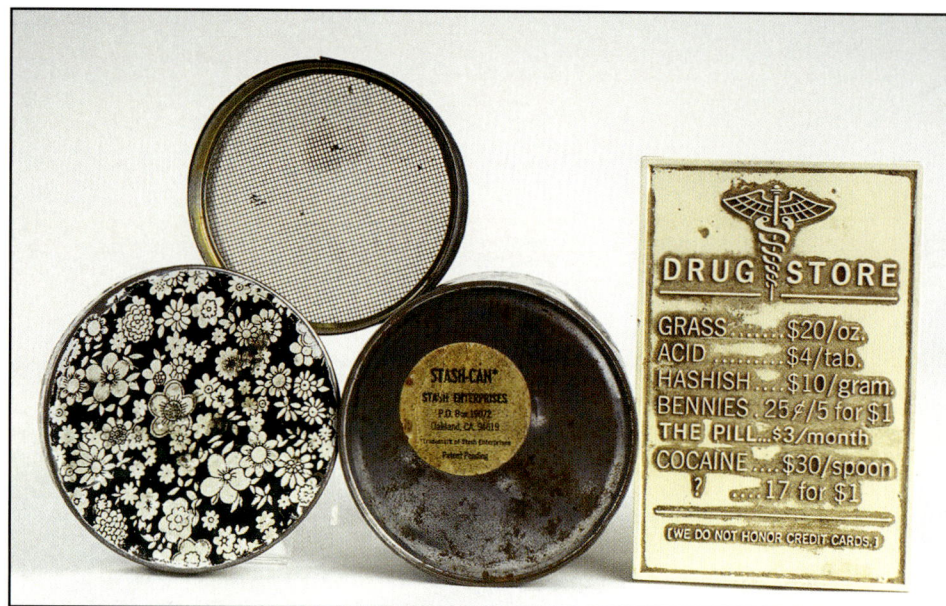

Rear: Ganja University T-shirt, c. 1970, scarce, $25-45. *Front from left:* brass belt buckle with hidden stash box and enamel butterfly design, c. 1968, scarce, $35-65; cigarette roller in original box for making "that perfect joint each and every time," common, $10-25. Original box adds fifty percent to value.

LSD poster "See Your Travel Agent" variations with implied reference to taking an "acid trip", scarce, $45-85. *Photograph courtesy of Walter "Hawkeye" Potaznick, West Bridgewater, MA.*

Poster, "Superior Acid Blows Your Mind," signed Moon 67, printed by American Newsrepeat Co., 243n Collins St., San Francisco, Ca, 28" h. x 22" w., 1967, rare, $75-175. Notice the image of a woman's head with long flowing hair in the upper left hand section of the smoke billowing from the swami's head.

33 1/3 LP album, *Overdose* and game board, Randor Records. Instructions advocate drug use with phrases like "No one who intends to stay straight may play," "sell 100 tabs of acid to narc, go to pen," "advance to Indian reservation, get wrecked on peyote," and "caught naked swimming with chick, pay $500 fine." Produced by Lumbee, 1970, rare, $50-100.

BuzzBee frisbee, manufactured by Altered Perceptions, Long Island, New York, rare, $100-250. In center of frisbee is a small hash pipe that a player might use before each throw. *Courtesy of Gary Sohmers, Wex Rex Collectibles, Hudson, MA.*

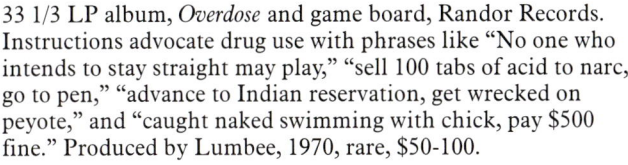

From left: R. Crumb pinback, "We're out of rolling papers," Rip Off Press, uncommon, $5-15; Humble Pie roach card flick book, printed in England, comical animated drug related cartoon, individual pages can be used to roll joints, rare, $50-100; "Smoke Grass" pinback, scarce, $15-35.

By 1965, various forms of both marijuana and LSD could be found throughout the country. Many young people rationalized drug use as a religious ceremony akin to the Native American Indians' use of peyote and mescaline. Popular author Aldous Huxley wrote in *The Doors of Perception*, about the way Native Americans experienced hallucinogenic, mind-expanding drugs to gain insight into the meaning of life. The rock band Jefferson Airplane refers to drug use in the song "White Rabbit" that opens with Grace Slick singing, *"One pill makes you larger and one pill makes you small."* Eventually this idealistic use of drugs gave way to recreational, although oftentimes harmful use that was not without dire consequences. Many talented musicians succumbed to the use of drugs. Jimi Hendrix died on September 18, 1970, and a month later Janis Joplin died of an overdose in a Hollywood hotel bathtub. In Paris a year later, Jim Morrison, lead singer of The Doors, also overdosed in a bathtub.

The last line of the Jefferson Airplane song "White Rabbit," states: *"...and the door mouse said, feed your head."* a possible reference to *Alice in Wonderland's* drug symbolism.

From left: pamphlet on drug facts for law enforcement, *LSD*, published by Los Angeles County Sheriff's Department, July 1967, 18 pages 11" h. x 8.5" w., scarce, $25-50; ceramic mushroom ashtray, Feed Your Head c. 1967, 6" h. x 5" w., scarce, $45-85 *Photograph courtesy of Walter "Hawkeye" Potaznick, West Bridgewater, MA.*

A Marijuana Day Smoke-In handbill was used to promote a National Marijuana Day Smoke-In concert and parade on April 29, 1973 in New York City. The flyer measures 8 1/2" x 11" and was printed by the event sponsor, the Youth International Party (YIP). One of YIP's subgroups was the White Panther Tribe whose leader, John Sinclair, was manager of the band MC5. The event consisted of a parade from Washington Square Park in Greenwich Village up Fifth Avenue to the Central Park bandstand. Here the crowd would be entertained by Apple recording artists Elephant's Memory and David Peel, and Teenage Lust. Mr. Marijuana (YIP's answer to Planter's Mr. Peanut) was the MC. The handbill also states that pre-rolled marijuana cigarettes would be distributed to the dope-hungry masses.

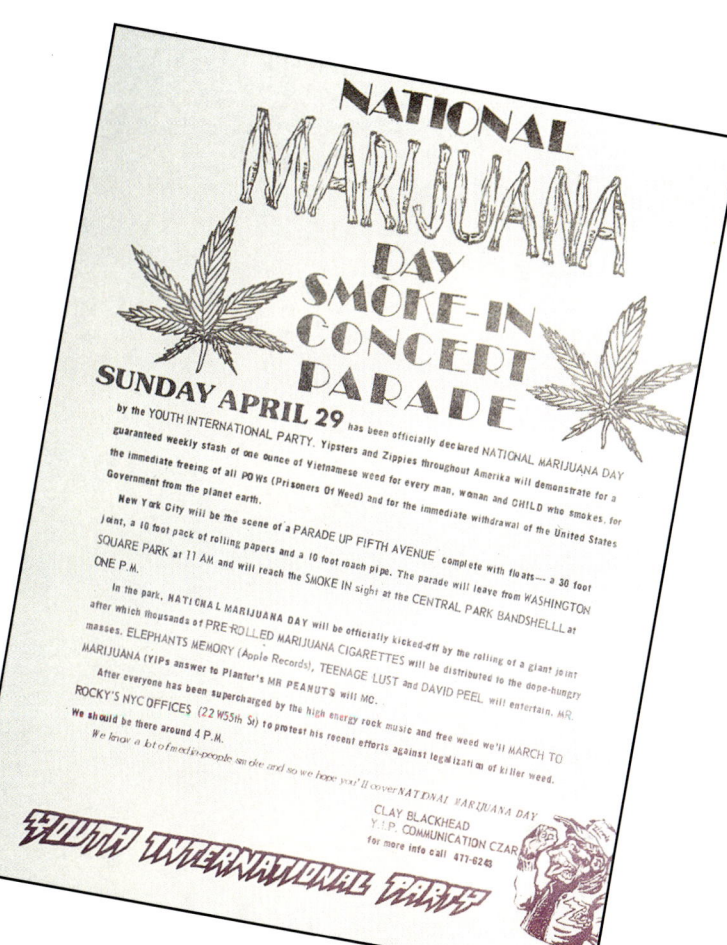

Handbill "National Marijuana Day Parade," sponsored by the Youth International Party, later known as "Yippies," inaugural year event, 11" h. x 8" w., 1971, scarce, $45-85.

Marijuana related booklets, sixteen to twenty pages each, published by Stone Kingdom Syndicate, several written by Mary Jane Superweed, 1970, original price $1, common, $15-35.

Satirical drug theme poster, "Vietnam Tea," scarce, $45-85.

Poster, "Free Wheelin' Franklin sez:" Franklin was one of the Fabulous Furry Freak Brothers, created by Gilbert Shelton, 23" h. x 19" w., 9-71, uncommon, $25-50.

Left rear and front: game of Grass burlap sack and cards, c. 1973, uncommon, $15-35. *Right rear:* ceramic vase with leather wrap around neck, raised Acapulco Gold leaf branch design, 12" h. x 6" w., c. 1968, very rare, $100-200. *Front center:* silver embossed marijuana leaf ring, common, $10-20. *Right front:* dice cube roach clip, common, $5-10.

All the items in the photo below refer to the shortlived craze of smoking the dried inside scrapings of banana peels to get high. This was popularized in the late 1960s song by Donovan, "Mellow Yellow."

Vinyl sticker and mailing postcard, Symbol Stix, Zig-Zag Man, Kaymac Distribution Systems, Royal Oak, MI, 1970, uncommon, $10-20.

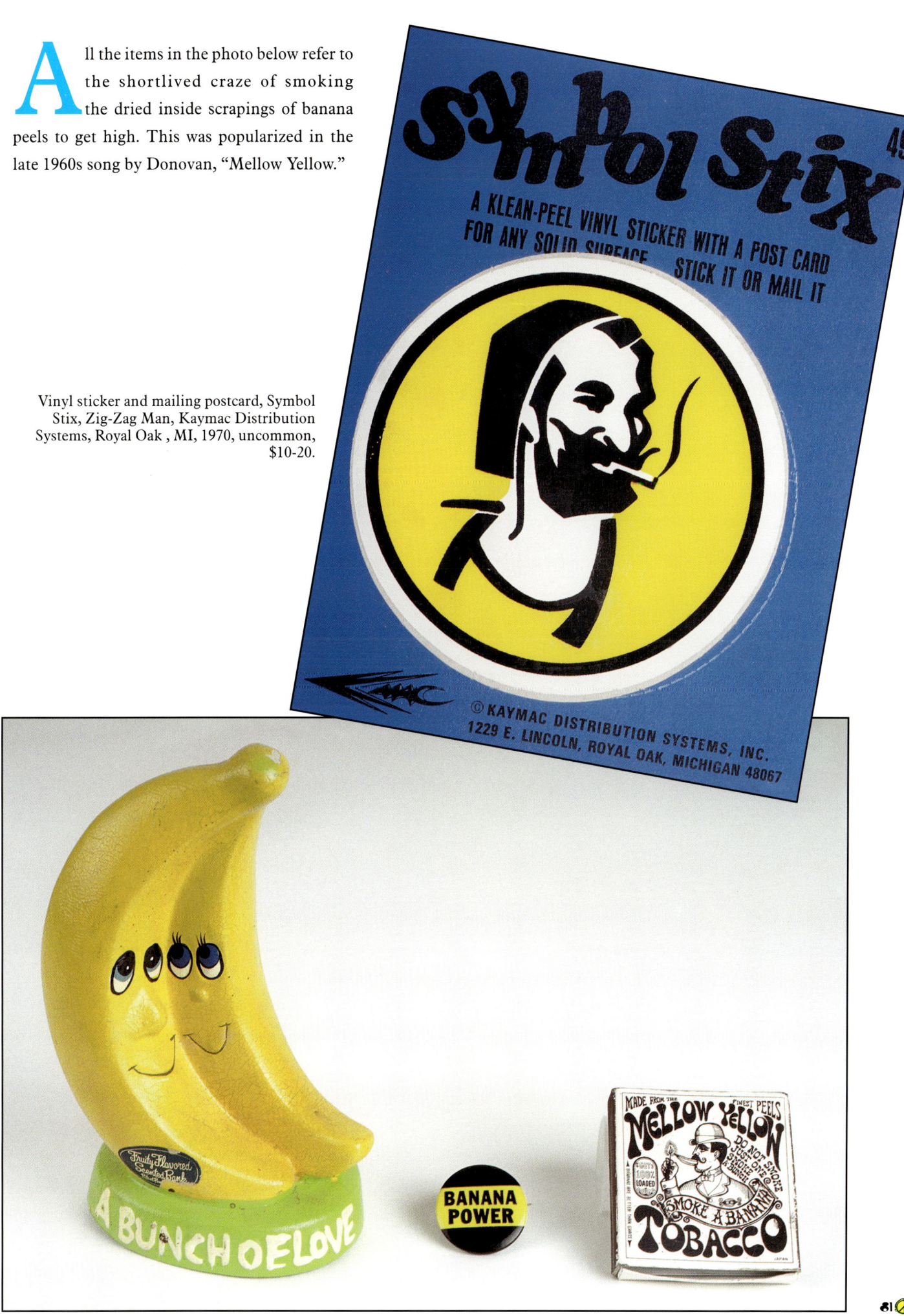

From left: metal canister with psychedelic mushroom motif, 8" h. x 4" w., common, $5-15; compilation book of avant-garde, hard core psychedelic music, *Mind Blowers*, 1969, uncommon, $10-25; fiberglass mushroom lamp shade with metal base, 11" h. x 7" w., c. 1967, scarce, $45-85.

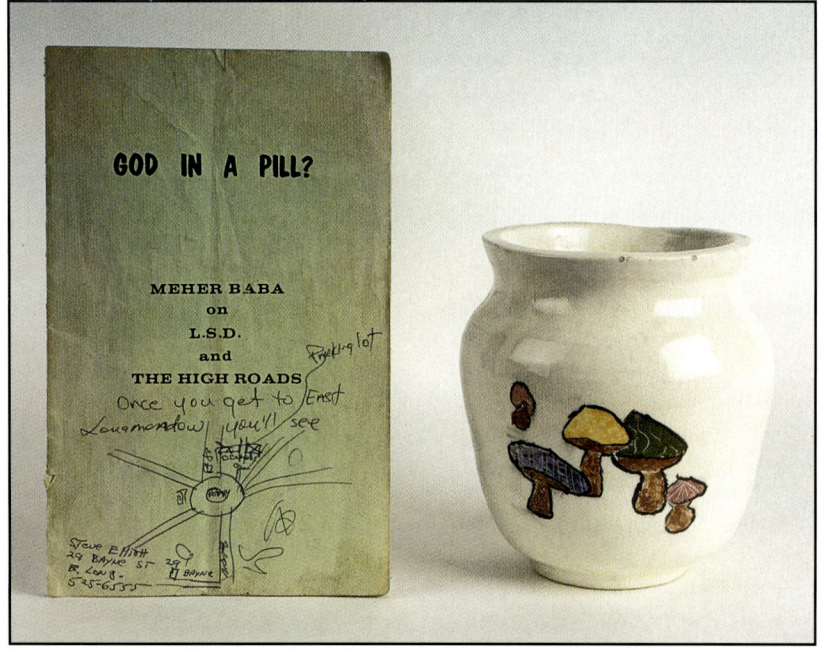

From left: pamphlet *God in a Pill?* on LSD and personal enlightenment through the use of psychedelic drugs. Written by Meher Baba and distributed at happenings, c. 1967, scarce, $35-65; ceramic bowl with hand painted psychedelic mushroom design, 6" h. x 5" w. scarce, $25-45. *Courtesy of Gary Moise, 70's-store.com, located at Orange Trading Co., Orange, MA.*

Back from left: bi-weekly underground newspaper, *Joint Issue*, v3 n12, Aug 14-Sep 21, 1972, E. Lansing, MI, scarce, $10-25; album by David Peel and the Lower Eastside, *Have a Marijuana*, 33 1/3 LP, copyright Nina Music, Elektra Records, c. 1968, common, $10-20. *Front row from left:* lampshade with popular slogan of the period about taking an LSD trip, 10" h. x 18" w., scarce, $25-50; metallic license plate with drug related play on words of Robert Crumb's well known slogan *Keep on Truckin'*, 7" h. x 14" w., uncommon, $10-25.

The Journal of Psychedelic Drugs was founded by David Smith, M.D., medical director of the Haight-Ashbury Free Clinic in 1967. It became a joint venture with the Student Association for the Study of Hallucinogens (STASH) of Madison, Wisconsin in 1970. The journal was distributed bi-annually and was considered the foremost publication of information on drugs, and drug use and abuse during the hippie period. The Haight-Ashbury Free Medical Clinic was the preeminent facility for the treatment of street related drug overdoses at the time. According to the editor's note, the purpose was "to compile and disseminate objective information relative to the various types of drugs used in the Haight-Ashbury subculture."

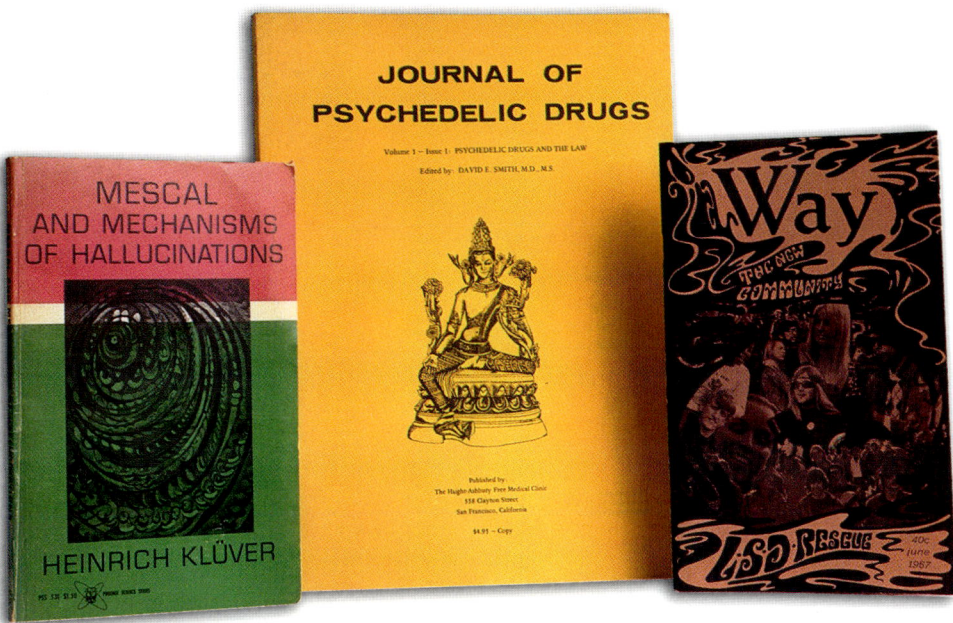

From left: text about peyote, *Mescal and Mechanisms of Hallucinations,* written by Heinrich Kluver, Phoenix Science Series, 1966, common, $10-20; *The Journal of Psychedelic Drugs,* v 1 n1 Summer 1967, uncommon, $15-35; monthly pamphlet size magazine, *Way,* published by Franciscan Fathers of California. This issue was dedicated to condemnation of the new drug culture and hippie lifestyle, June 1967, scarce, $10-20.

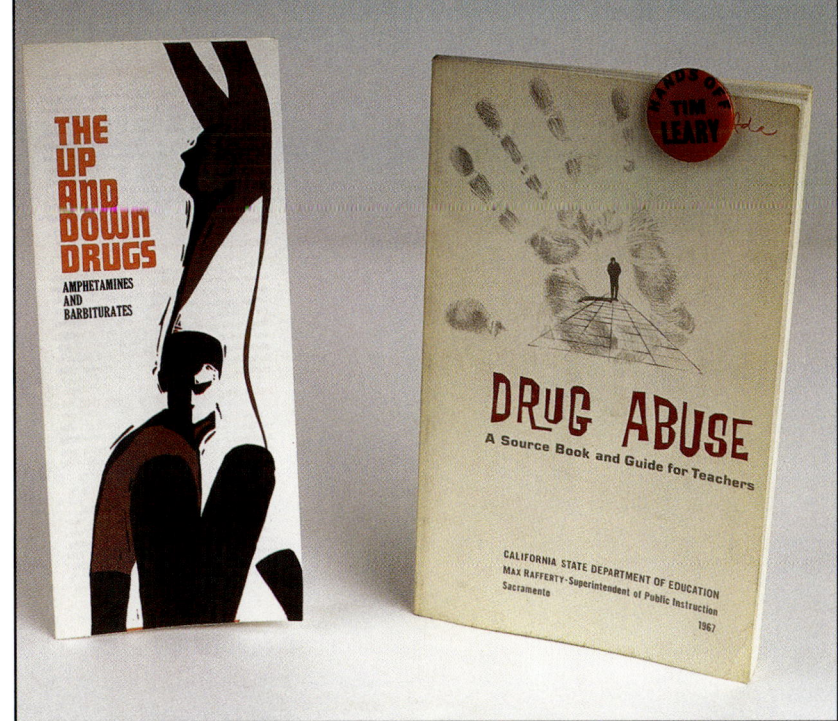

From left: educational pamphlet *The Up and Down Drugs,* published by the U.S. Department of Health and Human Services, 1968, common. $5-15; pinback, "Hands Off Tim Leary" scarce, $15-35; "Drug Abuse, a Source Book and Guide for Teachers," published by California Dept. of Education, 1967, uncommon, $10-25.

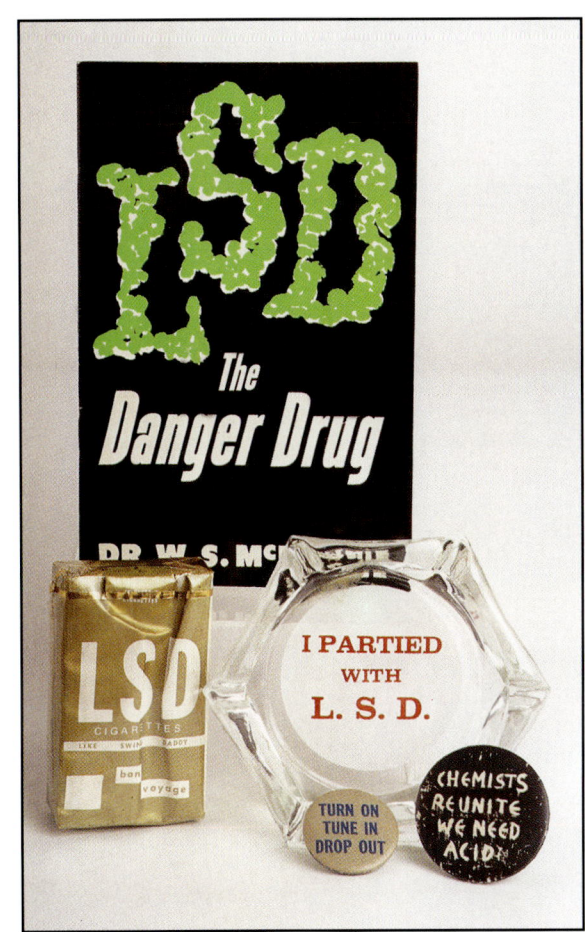

From top: propaganda pamphlet, *LSD-The Danger Drug,* Dr. W.S. McBirnie, 1968, uncommon, $25-50; pack of LSD (Like Swing Daddy) cigarettes, manufactured by Swinging Mothers Inc., Box 3795 Grand Central Station, NYC, 1967, very rare, $75-150; glass ashtray, "I Partied with L.S.D.", scarce, $25-50; pinback "Tune In, Turn On, Drop Out" (slogan attributed to Dr. Timothy Leary), common, $10-20; pinback "Druggists reunite-we need acid", scarce, $15-35.

From left: Avon candle box with psychedelic mushroom design, common, $5-15; metal serving tray with psychedelic mushroom design, 16" dia., uncommon, $15-35; vinyl purse with unusual colorful psychedelic mushroom design, c. 1967, 6" h. x 5.5" w., 11" long, rare, $45-85.

Top: brass marijuana leaf belt buckle, c. 1970, common, $10-25. *Center:* silver marijuana leaf pendant with rawhide necklace, common, $10-25. *Bottom from left:* embossed metal marijuana leaf belt buckle, common, $10-25; enamel cigarette case, with marijuana leaf design, scarce, $45-85; leather smoking accessories travel case with rolling papers, roach clip and stash compartment, uncommon, $10-25.

Lobby card from the popular cult movie *The Trip* starring Peter Fonda about an LSD experience, American International Pictures, 1967, common, $10-20.

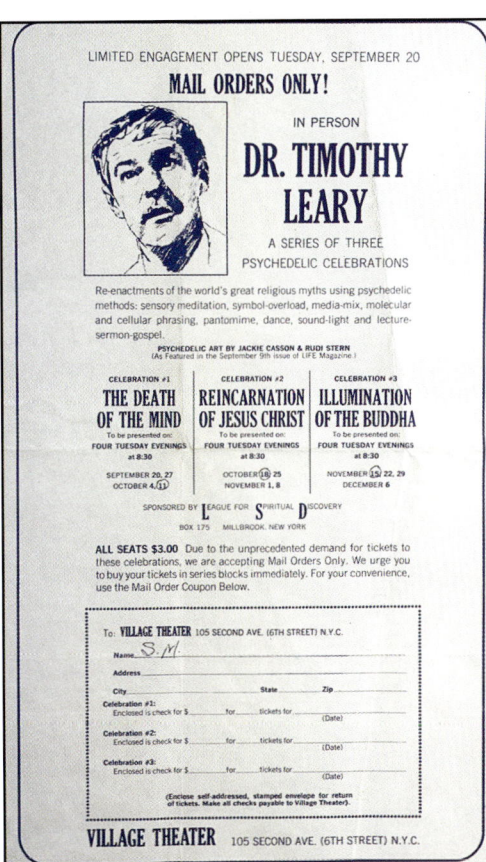

Handbill announcing a limited engagement psychedelic celebration given by Dr. Timothy Leary, PhD at the Village Theater, 105 Second Ave., New York City, 13" h. x 8" w., 1966, very rare, $150-250.

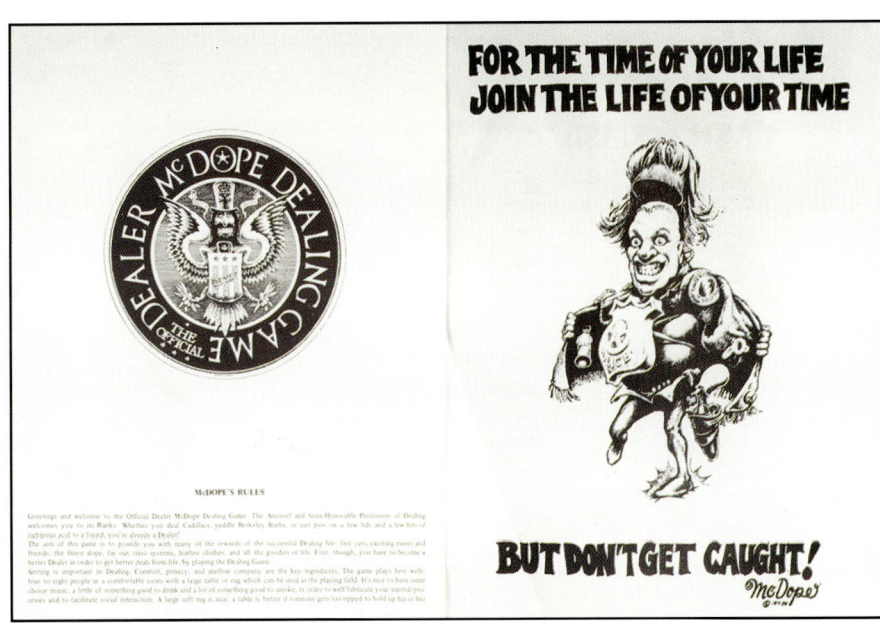

Instructions for playing *Dealer McDope Dealing Game*, copyright Dave Sheridan, Thom Patchett, 1971, rare, 1st edition $150-300; later versions dated 1977 and 1994 vary from $50-150.

Game board for *Dealer McDope Dealing Game*.

This very rare first edition guidebook was written by a new age religious order that subscribed to the spiritual use of psychedelic drugs. During the late 1960s, the Neo-American Church was one of four "quasi" religious organizations in the United States to use psychedelic substances as sacraments. Church leaders maintained that psychedelic substances were "divine sacraments, no matter who used them, in whatever spirit, and with whatever intention." The other three groups were the Church of the Awakening, the Native American Church, and the League for Spiritual Discovery.

Booklet, *The Psychedelic Guide to Preparation of the Eucharist*, how to prepare and perform a hallucinogenic drug experience, copyright Robert E. Brown, Neo American Church League for Spiritual Development, 59 pages, 11" h. x 8.5" w., 1968, very rare, first edition, $500-750; later editions, $250-400.

Inside pages of *The Psychedelic Guide to Preparation of the Eucharist*, the right side showing psychedelic peyote mushrooms as they appear in nature, and on the left, the chemical formula to synthesize mescaline, a hallucinogenic derivative of a cactus plant.

From left: paperweight, Trip or Trap, with comical drug related slogans, 1970, uncommon, $15-35; ceramic male hippie holding placard, "What a Trip", 1968, Enesco, 6" h. common, $10-25; stoneware novelty canister labeled LSD, 7" h. uncommon, $25-50; ceramic female hippie holding placard, "You Turn Me On", 1968, Enesco, 6" h., common, $10-25; pinback "You Turn Me On", 1968, 2" dia., common, $5-15.

Poster #409, "Be Hip," Today's Army, Synergisms, San Francisco, 32" h. x 20" w., 1971, common, $15-35.

Flocked black light poster #116, "Keep A' Puffin," Straight Arrow Productions, 35" h. x 23" w., 1972, uncommon, $25-50.

Poster #292 "Pipe Dream," artist Lawrence LeClair, Personality Posters, Inc. 74 Fifth Ave., New York City, 21" h. x 28" w., 1967, scarce, $50-100.

Press book for *The Acid Eaters*, a "B" cult movie, uncommon, $15-30.

Poster "Rapid Transit", Petagno III, Saladin Productions, Los Angeles, 34" h. x 23" w., 1970, scarce, $50-100.

Tie-dyed necktie with hand blocked marijuana leaf design, scarce, $15-35.

Hand tooled leather purse with embossed psychedelic mushroom design, made in Mexico, uncommon, $35-65. Similar purses (not shown) with flower power design are common and often found from $15-35 depending on detail and color.

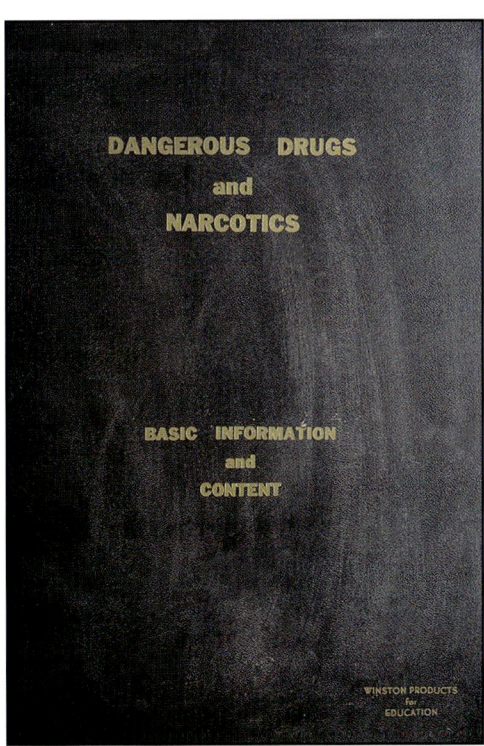

Oversize flip chart book, *Dangerous Drugs and Narcotics*, published by Winston Products for Education, 32" h. x 18" w., c. 1967, scarce, $50-100.

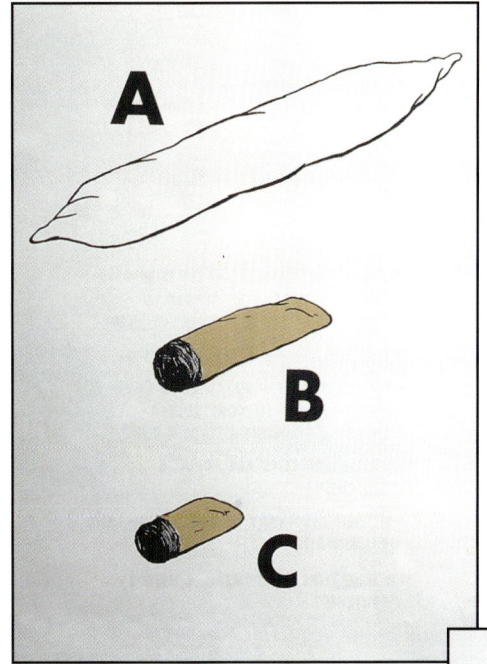

Page from *Dangerous Drugs and Narcotics*, with images of a joint in various stages of having been smoked.

Page from *Dangerous Drugs and Narcotics*, describing marijuana cigarette using interesting terminology.

- MARIJUANA CIGARETTE WRAPPED IN BROWN CIGARETTE PAPERS
- MARIJUANA CIGARETTE WRAPPED IN WHITE PAPER
  - MARIJUANA CIGARETTES VARY IN SIZE AND SHAPE
  - THE ENDS ARE TWISTED OR TUCKED IN SO AS TO PREVENT LOSS OF LOOSE MARIJUANA
- A MARIJUANA CIGARETTE WHICH IS LARGER THAN THE AVERAGE ONE IS CALLED A "BOMBER"
- REGULAR COMMERCIAL CIGARETTE SHOWN FOR COMPARISON PURPOSES

KNOWN AS
- REEFERS   • J'S   • JOINTS
- STICKS   • NUMBERS

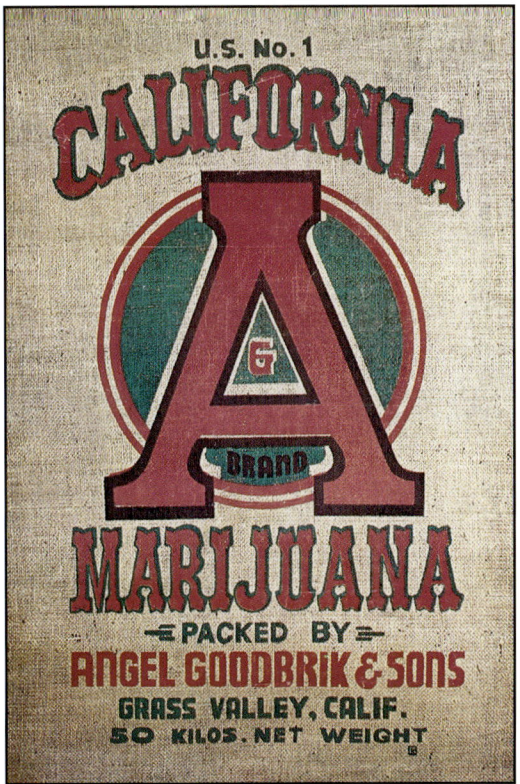

Poster "California Brand Grade A Marijuana," Sunset Marketing, Los Angeles, 34" h. x 23" w., 1971, uncommon, $15-35.

- D-LYSERGIC ACID DIETHYLAMIDE TARTRATE (LSD 25)
- COLORLESS, TASTELESS, AND ODORLESS
- HALLUCINOGENIC-PSYCHODELIC TYPE DRUG
  - LIQUID FORM
  - SOMETIMES PLACED ON SUGAR CUBES
  - CRYSTALLINE FORM WHICH IS SOMETIMES PACKAGED IN CAPSULES
  - SOMETIMES IN TABLETS

COMMON TERMINOLOGY
- LSD: "ACID", "25", "THE BEAST"
- USER: "ACID HEAD"
- BAD EXPERIENCE: "FREAK OUT", "BAD TRIP", "BUM TRIP"
- TAKING LSD: "TURNING ON"
- UNDER INFLUENCE OF LSD: "TRIP"

Page from *Dangerous Drugs and Narcotics*, describing LSD using interesting terminology.

*F*eds 'n' Heads was initially an underground comic book created by Gilbert Shelton in 1968 that featured Wonder Wart-Hog–The Hog of Steel, and the Fabulous Furry Freak Brothers.

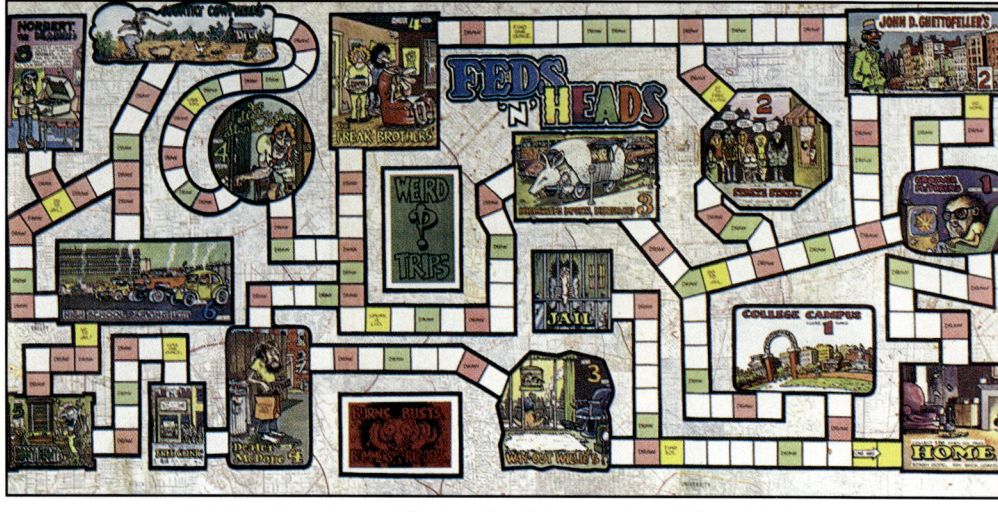

Fold out board game *"Feds n' Heads"*, created by Gilbert Shelton. This game appeared in a 1971 issue of Playboy magazine, common, $10-25.

"Drug Abuse" handbill, using psychedelic artwork; identifies warning signs and side effects of illicit drugs, printed by Gassen Drug Stores, 11" h. x 8.5" w., c. 1970, uncommon, $10-25.

Handbill, advertising a "Smoke In" rally, 11" h. x 8" w., c. 1969, scarce, $35-65.

Pipe belt buckle, brass filigree design, 2.5" h. x 3.5" w., 1973, uncommon, $35-65. *Pipe and photograph courtesy of Walter "Hawkeye" Potaznick, West Bridgewater, MA.*

Chapter Five
Psychedelectibles

Fabric with op art psychedelic design images, cotton, c. 1968, rare, $45-85 per yard. Textile prices vary with design and amount of available yardage. Known designer fabrics are $50-100 per yard, varied multiple graphic designs are $25-50 per yard, and simple floral or geometric patterns are $5-25 per yard.

The term "psychedelics" in the late 1960s applied to objects that ranged from drugs to music to art. Among the psychedelic poster artists working in the San Francisco area in the late 1960s, five of the better known were Victor Moscoso, Stanley Mouse, Rick Griffin, Alton Kelley, and Wes Wilson. Moscoso was best known for posters that changed colors under different illumination and "black lighting," while Wilson used a flowing Art Nouveau style similar to early 1900s European posters. All of these artists produced artwork and graphics for concert posters, record album covers, books, and underground comics. In New York, Peter Max became the most commercially successful poster artist in the country applying his psychedelic technique of brightly colored, stark images to textiles and household accessories.

The majority of psychedelic bands were found on the East and West coasts. They had names like West Coast Pop Art Experimental Band, Question Mark and the Mysterians, Seeds, 13th Floor Elevators, Vanilla Fudge, Moby Grape, Mandrake Memorial, Pearls Before Swine, Big Brother and the Holding Company, and The Doors to name a few. The Cream's 1968 *Wheels of Fire* album was the first platinum album in the music industry.

Poster, "Drop In To The Other Culture", 25" h. x 20" w., artist and publisher unknown, c. 1966, scarce, $50-100.

Peter Max Book Covers, Westab Inc., Dayton, OH, 15" h. x 10" w. 1970, uncommon, $15-35.

Innerspace, the Magazine of the Psychedelic Community, 1966, newsstand price 50 cents, Box 212 Old Chelsea Sta., NY, NY 10011, uncommon, $10-20.

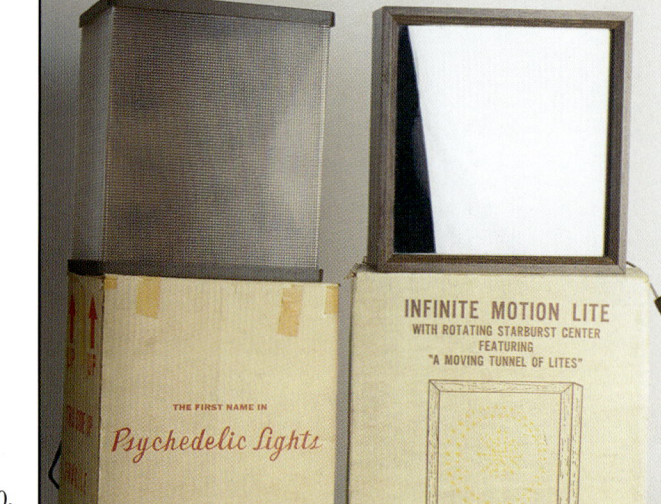

From left: Infinite Motion Lite, Lava Simplex, Chicago, c. 1970, scarce, $50-100; Psychedelic Lights, Ames Electronics, Culver City, CA, 1969, for home use to "help blow your mind", scarce, $50-100.

From left: Honey Light, plastic table top motion lamp, M.S.I., New York, 7.5" h. x 6" w., common, $5-15; Psychostrobe, metal electronic strobe light, Science Fair, 6" h. x 4" w., scarce, $35-65.

From left: psychedelic electric circular motion disc, 16" dia., scarce, $50-100; psychedelic swirl glass dish, 10" dia., uncommon, $35-65. *Courtesy of Gary Moise, 70's-store.com at Orange Trading Company, Orange, MA.*

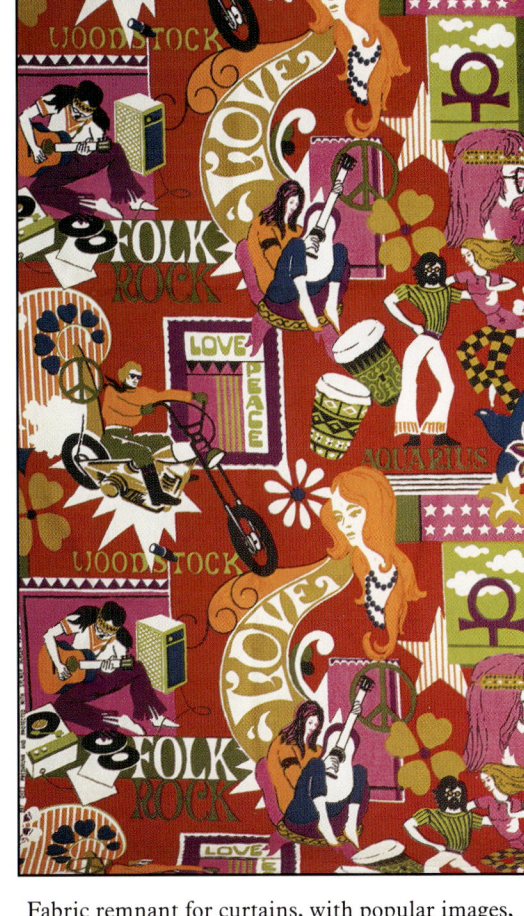

Fabric remnant for curtains, with popular images, uncommon, $15-35 per yard.

Nehru collar bell sleeve evening shirt, psychedelic paisley design, formal attire for happenings, with oversize embossed metal buttons, Revelations, Inc., 1967, rare, $65-125.

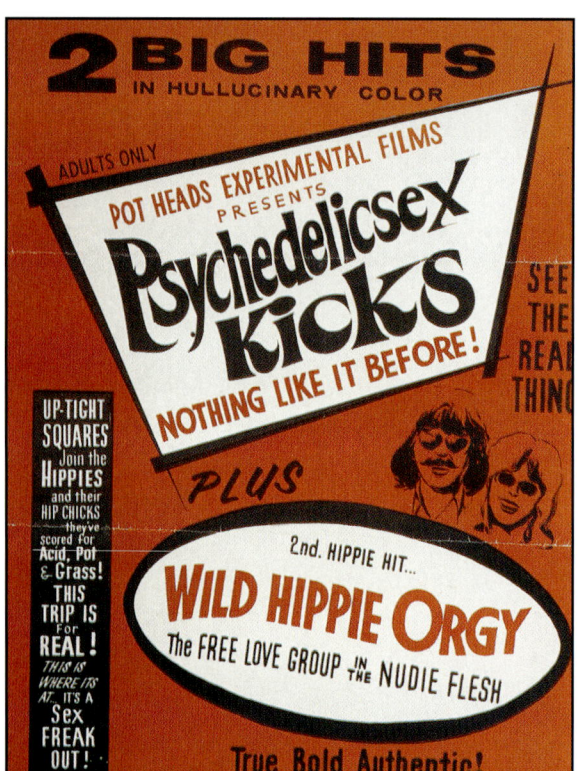

Tri-fold movie brochure promoting grade "B" cult movies *Psychedelicsex Kicks* and *Wild Hippie Orgy,* Gillman Film Corp., Los Angeles, CA, 11" h. x 8.5" w., 1968, uncommon, $10-25.

One sheet poster for the Beatles movie *Yellow Submarine,* United Artists, 1968, scarce, $200-300.

Psychedelic Art, Electric Tibet, designer Tom Weller, Joyful Wisdom Enterprises, art show opening May 1, Berkeley CA, 19" h. x 13" w., 1967, common, $20-40.

Capital Records album insert poster, 20" h. x 12" w., 1967, common, $15-35.

Center: psychedelic poster, man smoking hookah, published by Hi Sun, 22" h. x 14" w., scarce, $35-65. *Front:* ceramic handled coffee mugs with psychedelic design, Holt-Howard, 4.5" h. x 3.5" w., 1968, uncommon, $15-35.

From left: book, *Psychedelic Prayers*, by Timothy Leary, publisher New York University Books, New Hyde Park, 1966, cover drawing by Michael Bowen, common, $20-45; Psychedelic Scent Legal Pot novelty, H. X Fishlove & Co., Chicago, 1968, uncommon, $5-15; vinyl 3 ring binder with psychedelic design, c. 1967, uncommon, $10-25.

35mm rotating disc used to create a light show, each slide projects a different psychedelic image and effect when projected onto a wall or ceiling, c. 1967, rare, $20-45.

Psychedelic design book cover, "Rap Wrap," artwork Gene Bellos, copyright by Lettuce, 1970, common, $2-5.

Three posters/book covers, "Sok-It-Delic," take off on the *Laugh In* television show slogan "sock it to me" combined with the word psychedelic, Col Ad, Buffalo, NY, 12.5" h. x 11" w., uncommon, $10-25.

Record album, *Music For Longhairs*, 33 1/3 LP, Design Records, uncommon, $10-20.

The Psychedelic Coloring Book, Larry Bowser, Hallmark Cards Inc., 5.5" h. x 4" w. 1971, uncommon, $10-20.

Child's charm bracelet on original card entitled Psychedelic, c.1967, scarce, $20-45.

From left: vinyl three ring binder and tote bag, Jet Set, psychedelic astrological graphics, 14" h. x 16" w., uncommon, $20-45; psychedelic crepe paper party decoration ribbon, Dennison, c. 1967, uncommon, $3-6; metallic hand held mirror and hairbrush set with psychedelic swirl design, uncommon, $15-35.

Vinyl overnight suitcase with psychedelic design, 14" h. x 22" w. c. 1966, scarce, $35-65.

Top: massage oil bottles with Peter Max designed label, ISKCON Corp., 2.5" h. x 1.5" w., 1973, scarce, $20-45. *Bottom from left:* Hot Shots candy with psychedelic pinwheel design, uncommon, $5-10; hippie lipstick with original box, common, $5-10; wristwatch with central moving flower power swirl design, Le Jour Time Co., scarce, $35-65.

Top: alarm clock radio with unusual psychedelic design using the word "clock" and a pointing finger, General Electric, 5" h. x 7" w., 1969, rare, $75-150. *Bottom from left:* vinyl eight track tape carry case with Peter Max-like design, 5" h. x 6" w., rare, $65-125; Dominoes with iridescent color and box design, Fitz and Floyd, Dallas, uncommon, $20-45.

Canadian Pacific Railway brochure, psychedelic design, 1968, uncommon, $5-10.

Paint-a Poster by the Numbers, #1203, "Button Button," featuring hippie chicks and pinbacks, Art Award Co., North Bergen NJ, 11" h. x 3" dia., 1968, scarce, $35-65.

33 1/3 LP record album, *More Psychedelic Guitars*, Custom Records, c. 1968, uncommon, $10-20.

From left: psychedelic paisley enameled metal belt buckle, c. 1966, scarce, $20-45; painted wood bracelet, c. 1971, uncommon, $10-25. *Photograph courtesy of Walter "Hawkeye" Potaznick, West Bridgewater, MA.*

Chapter Six
Crash Pad

From left: molded fiberglass table lamp, 14" h., c. 1967, scarce, $45-85; lava lamp with original box, made by Lava Lite Corp., c. 1967, uncommon, $50-100, original box adds 50% to value of item. *Courtesy of Gary Moise, 70's-store.com at Orange Trading Company, Orange, MA.*

Milk glass night light, "Let Love Shine" 6" h. x 4.5" w., c. 1967, uncommon, $25-45.

Many so-called hippies were children of affluent parents, rebelling against their conservative upbringings, while at the same time developing a sense of their own lifestyles. One of the more unusual crash pads for American hippies could be found on the far side of the island of Mykonos in Greece. During the summer of 1972 many hippies lived in tiny caves that dotted the shoreline of this deserted mountainous area.

In the early 1970s, many hardcore hippies became disillusioned with the commercialism that began to be associated with the movement. These were the dropouts that sought refuge in the rural communes of the "back-to-the-land movement." These refugees returned to basic group living conditions as a means to continue their search for the meaning of life. Well known communes of the time were The Diggers, The Hog Farm, Drop City, and Free Spirit. Both "Jesus Freaks" and "Hare Krishnas" were lifestyle variations of the same theme evolving from a search for universal truth. The artistry of everyday household items became one way of expressing their beliefs. Living off the land and the use of recycled decorative items were popular trends.

Wood bead hanging curtain, 72" h. x 36" w., c. 1967, uncommon, $35-65.

Environmental protest metal trash basket, maker unknown, 12" h. x 10" w., c. 1969, rare, $45-85. *Photograph courtesy of Walter "Hawkeye" Potaznick, Bridgewater, MA.*

Formica end table, butterfly and marijuana leaf design, 24" square, c. 1966, rare, $45-85.

Pop art Andy Warhol-like cushions, household commodities design, 18" h. x 8" w., c. 1967, scarce, $35-65.

Left and right: hippie and flower child ceramic liquor bottles, Royal Enfield Porcelain, 12" h. x 4" w., 1968, common, $10-20 each; *Center:* plastic beads for decorating and wearing, Coast Creative Industries, Chatsworth, CA, 1972, uncommon, $25-50 per bag.

Gary Moise, survivor of the hippie period, friend of the author, owner of Orange Trading Co., and 70's store.com among the many hippie period items for sale in his Orange, MA warehouse.

Hand woven wall art, wool, 34" h. x 24" w., scarce, $75-150. *Courtesy of Gary Moise, 70's-store.com at Orange Trading Company, Orange, MA.*

Left and right: string art sculptures, uncommon, $25-50. *Center:* hand formed, lighted sculptural lamp, clear lucite on wood base, Lights Fantastic, 16" h. x 6" w., c. 1966, scarce, $50-100. *Courtesy of Gary Moise, 70's-store.com at Orange Trading Company, Orange, MA.*

Aquarian Age sleeping bag, note use of Woodstock name to target young customers, c. 1971, uncommon, $25-50.

Love Lite motion lamp, Love Lite Lamps, 12" h. x 5" dia., Chicago, 1973, uncommon, $25-50.

From left: very intricate macramé plant holder, 26" h. x 8" w., scarce, $65-125; hemp wall hanging, uncommon, $50-100. *Courtesy of Gary Moise, 70's-store.com, located at Orange Trading Company, Orange, MA.*

Rear: 33 1/3 and 45 rpm record album cases, Platter-Pak, 1966, common, $15-35; *Front:* Radio Phono, Sears, 1968, uncommon, $35-65.

Wallpaper with pop art psychedelic design, c. 1967, scarce, $100 per roll. Price varies with visual appeal and amount available, $25-125 per roll.

Psychedelic design blanket, cotton, c. 1969, uncommon, $35-65.

From left: banana bicycle seat, psychedelic design, Beacon, 1972, scarce, $35-65; bread and bun warmer, Kaz Heating Products, New York City, c. 1967, scarce, $35-65; black and white psychedelic swirl paper lampshade, uncommon, $10-20; Electric Psychedelic Love Lamp, c. 1972, scarce, $45-85.

From left: chip and dip serving bowls with flower power design, glass and brass, c. 1967, scarce, $35-65; cotton beach towel, design has flower power hippie girl in forefront and rock band in background, uncommon, c. 1966, $10-25; flower power plastic wastebasket, 16" h. x 10" w., c. 1967, common, $5-15.

Wall hanging, wood carved spokes, woven wool outer ring, inner pottery smiling sun, 28" dia., c. 1967, scarce, $45-85.

From left: 16-month calendar, "Ralph" Sept. 1967-Dec. 1968, Hallmark, 12" h. x 9" w., rare, $35-65; 1969 calendar – each month a different psychedelic or op art design, Polfa, Poland, 18" h. x 12" w., rare, $50-100. *Photograph courtesy of Walter "Hawkeye" Potaznick, West Bridgewater, MA.*

Beach towel with hippie graphics, cotton, summer 1973, uncommon, $10-25.

Plastic kitchen tray, 18" h. x 22" w., c. 1967, uncommon, $10-20.

From left: American flag design suede moccasin style shoes, scarce, $45-85; American flag design candlestick telephone, American Telecommunications Corp., 1973, scarce, $75-150; American flag design suede purse, scarce, $35-65.

The San Francisco and Bay Area People's Yellow Pages No. 3, copyright and distributed by The People's Yellow Pages Collective, 10.5" h. x 8" w., 169 pages, 1973, very rare, $100-200.

Booklet, *On Chanting the Hare Krishna,* 13 pages, printed by ISKCON (International Society for Krishna Consciousness) Press, Boston, 1968, uncommon, $10-25.

From left: Sri Isopanishad, Swami Prabhupada, 1970, common, $10-20; ceramic guru figurine with peace symbol necklace, Chadwick Miller Inc., 1970, 5" h. x 3" w., uncommon, $20-45; Guru game, made by Lowe, 14" h. x 12" w., 1970, common, $10-20.

Quarterly magazine of commune living, *Free Spirit Press*, v1 n4, 1972, uncommon, $10-25.

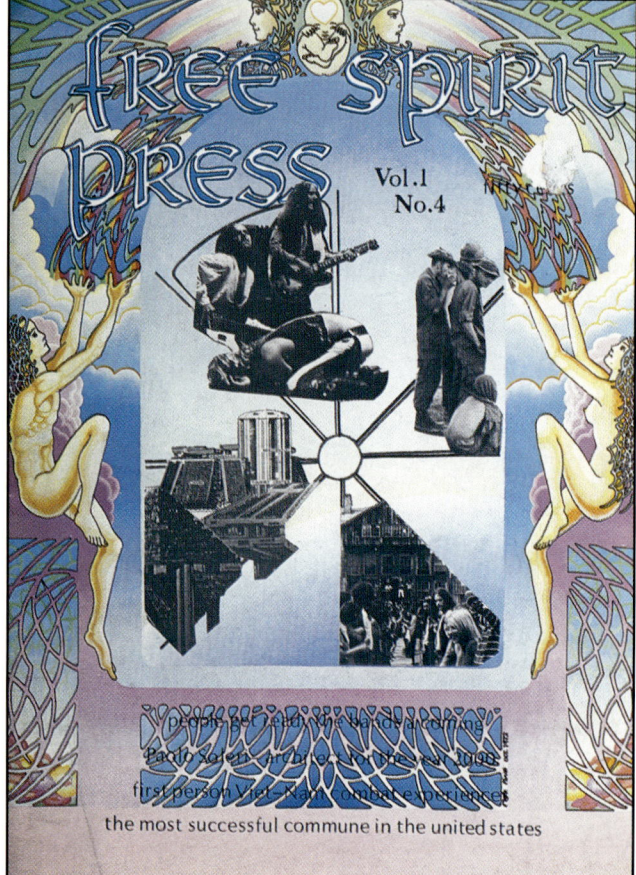

LP, 33 1/3, record album, *Spirit in Flesh*, jacket photo of the Brotherhood of the Spirit commune and members, one of the most successful communes in the USA, located in Warwick, MA, c. 1973, uncommon, $10-25. *Courtesy of Gary Moise, 70's-store.com, located at Orange Trading Company, Orange, MA.*

From left: matching vinyl carry all and cooler with popular hippie slogans and graphics, Nappy, Farmingdale, NJ, 1972, scarce, $25-45 each; wire and glass bead incense or candle holder, S.N.K. Enterprises, Inc., 5" dia., uncommon, $10-25; Little Smiles coasters, Executive Games, Inc., 1971, uncommon, $5-15.

From left: vinyl hairnet box, Twiggy-like silhouette, uncommon, $25-45; Electric Flower lighted wall mirror in original box, Mirror Go Lightly, uncommon, $25-45; Flower is Power comic button in original package, 2" dia., common, $5-15; visor mirror, uncommon, $10-25. *Courtesy of Gary Moise, 70's-store.com at Orange Trading Company, Orange, MA.*

Motorcycle peace symbol sissy bar, chrome back support for rear passenger, 26" high, 16" wide, c. 1967, scarce, $25-$50.

Leather carry bag with an abstract American flag design using peace symbol and map, 8" diameter, wide handle strap with alternating peace symbols and marijuana leaves, 22" long, c. 1973, rare, $50-$100. *Photograph courtesy of Walter "Hawkeye" Potaznick, West Bridgewater, MA.*

Chapter Seven
Flower Power

The term "flower power" described hippie ideas and behavior as early as 1962 when Beat poet and antiwar activist Allen Ginsberg used it to describe how the power of nature could defeat war. At an October 1967 march on Washington, protesters placed flowers in the rifle barrels of National Guardsmen urging them to put down their guns. During the mid 1960s, hippies were referred to as flower children, but within a few years the meaning became more pervasive, appearing in household designs, clothing and decorative items.

Box top display card "Flower Children Bubble Gum," with image of rock band and guru surrounded by a psychedelic wave, Leaf Brands, W. R. Grace & Co. Chicago, IL, 6" h. x 5" w., c. 1967, uncommon, $10-25.

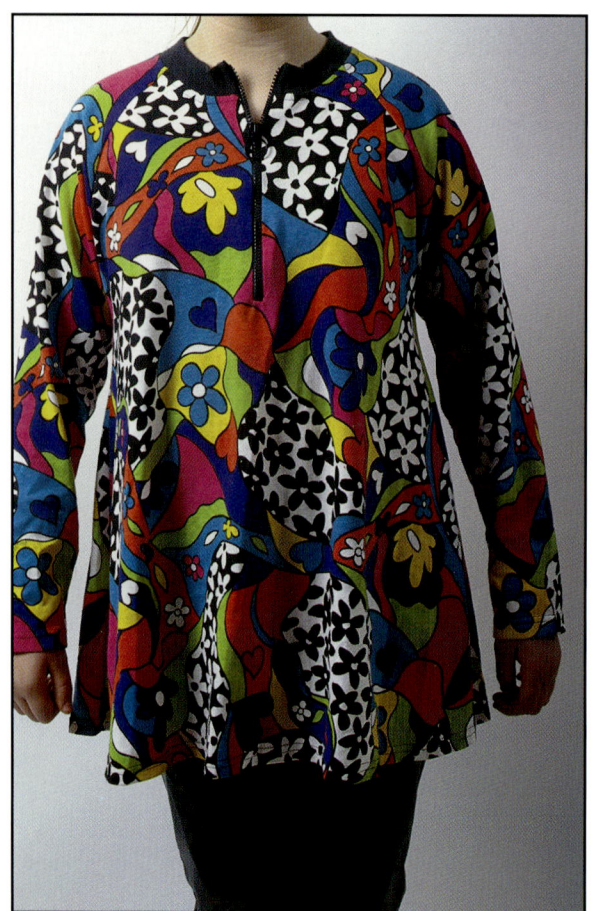

Rear: Flower power vinyl overnight case, 16" dia., c. 1967, uncommon, $15-35. *Center:* two small hard plastic dolls, common, $5-15. *Front from left:* "POP" vinyl inflatable flower power design hangers, common, $10-20; flower power design clogs with leather upper and wood bottom, c. 1972, scarce, $25-45.

Flower power shirt, pull chain metal zipper, cotton, common, $10-25.

Cotton dress with large flower power design and bat wing sleeves, c. 1967, uncommon, $10-25.

Flower power shirt, cotton, common, $10-25.

Rear from left: vinyl carry bag, 17" h. x 11" w., c. 1966, common, $5-15; Posy Pitch ring toss game, 16" h. x 12" w., Eagle Rubber Co., Ashland, OH, 1971, uncommon, $15-35. *Front from left:* flower power nylon hat, c. 1966, uncommon, $15-35; metal painted civil defense hat decorated with flower power stickers and used for protection against police batons in protest rallies, c. 1966, rare, $35-65.

From left: instant hairset and curlers, "Up-Beat," with flower power lunchbox and plastic cover, Sears, June, 27, 1969, uncommon, $25-50; flower power porcelain table top cigarette lighter, OMC, 4" h. x 2" dia., uncommon, $10-25; portable household file, Ballonoff Metal Products, Cleveland, 10" h. x 12" w., 6" deep, c. 1967, common, $10-20.

From left: vinyl flower power waste basket, c. 1968, common, $5-15; flower power invitation cards, Valiant Publishing Ltd., uncommon, $5-10; vinyl flower power purse, uncommon, $15-35; Betty Lou cosmetic bag, c. 1967, common, a variety of cosmetic products was sold under the "Betty Lou" label, $5-15.

From left: banana seat for bicycle, scarce, c. 1971, $35-65; decks of playing cards with psychedelic flower power design, common, $5-15; scale with flower power motif, Brearly Corp., Rockford, IL, 1968, scarce, $35-65.

From left: glass Smiley Face flower in vase, New Designs, Inc., 1969, common, $10-20; magnetic wallboard with flower power design, c 1968, Takahashi, San Francisco, uncommon, $10-25; lucite coaster set, copyright Colorflo, 1970, uncommon, $15-35; wood flower power desktop cardholder, Fitz and Floyd, 1969, uncommon, $15-35; glass ashtray made by Higgins, 6" h. x 8" w. c. 1966, scarce, $75-150.

From left: "Paint Kit" facial and body paint set, Fabergé, 1967, scarce, $15-35; Murano glass flower power bead bracelet, c. 1968, uncommon, $10-20; vinyl flower power eyeglass case, uncommon, $5-15; Avon bottle Volkswagen hippie van, common, $5-10.

Ron Jon Surf Shop cotton flower power design T-shirt, 1967, rare, $45-85.

From left: flower power metal wall clock, Spartus Corp., 10" dia., c. 1967, common, $15-30; handmade rainbow design wax candles, common, $5-10 each; rainbow design shag sofa pillow, 20"square, c.1967, common, $5-15.

Roll of flower power wall paper, c. 1967, common, $10-25 per roll.

Cotton flower power hand towel, 18" h. x 12" w., c.1967, common, $5-15.

Sleeping bag with flower power design and hippie slogans, c. 1967, uncommon, $25-50.

From left: Memories, high school year book with flower power design cover, 1968, scarce, $35-65; Murano glass floral bead bracelet, uncommon, $10-25; "flower power" transistor radio, Windsor, 1969, scare, $35-75.

"Rickie Tickie Stickies," original package, 1968, common, $5-15 per pack.

Flower power cotton child's dress, c. 1967, common, $10-20.

Shirt with the word "flower power" repeating design, cotton, no label, c. 1967, uncommon, $15-35. *Photograph courtesy of Walter "Hawkeye" Potaznick, West Bridgewater, MA.*

Songs to Sing in San Francisco, MCA Music, 4 perforated attached sheets, 22" h. x 16" w., 1967, scarce, $35-65. *Photograph courtesy of Walter "Hawkeye" Potaznick, West Bridgewater, MA.*

Chapter Eight
Heading in the Right Direction

The local "head shop" was the place to purchase drug paraphernalia, black light posters, underground news, and the latest style rags (a popular term for clothing). The Rag Barrier in Manchester, New Hampshire was one such place. Other imaginative monikers were Grass is Greener in Salisbury Beach, New Hampshire, Elysian Fields in the Georgetown area of Washington, D.C., and Psychedelicatessen in New York City.

Blacklight dealer store display kit, contains a dozen tube lights and table top stand-up advertising poster. Blacklight was used to illuminate psychedelic wall posters with special fluorescent effects, Westinghouse, 1972, rare, $75-150.

From left: LSD (Like Swing Daddy) cigarettes, Swinging Mothers Inc., Box 3795 Grand Central Sta., NYC, 1967, very rare, $75-150; Peace lights, dove with olive branch image on pack, made in Japan, scarce, $35-65.

From left: leather trivet with hand tooled and painted marijuana leaf, uncommon, $10-25; store box of Zig-Zag rolling papers, common $10-25; ceramic bottle with leather neck grip and molded image of Zig-Zag man, 12" h. x 6" w., c. 1968, very rare, $100-250; counter top stoneware bust of Zig-Zag man, 6" h. x 4" w., rare, $100-150.

From left: Spiro Agnew rolling papers dispenser, scarce, $35-65; individual packs $5-10; Bambu advertising butane lighter, c. 1968, common, $5-15; small hookah, 8" h., uncommon, $25-50; 4 piece take-apart brass pipe made with concealed stash compartment for traveling across borders, 1968, scarce, $50-100.

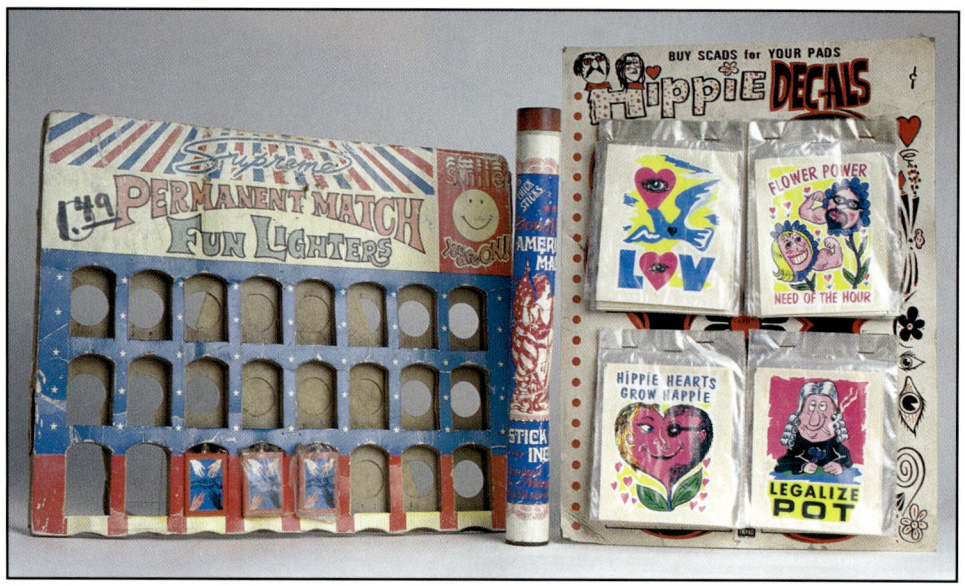

From left: butane lighter store display for the unity lighter "Reach Out for Your Brother", Supreme, c. 1967, rare, $150-300; individual lighters $10-20; Miss Liberty incense sticks canister, uncommon, $5-15; cardboard stand-up counter top store display with four different hippie decals, 20" h. x 14" w., c. 1967, scarce, $75-150, individual decals $2-3.

From left: plastic peace sign keychain counter top store display, scarce, $50-100; individual key chains $5-10; leather peace sign hair barrette burlap wall hanging store display, uncommon, $35-65; individual barrettes $5-10; Freshmor peace symbol air freshener store wall display, c. 1967, rare, $65-125 complete; individual fresheners $3-5.

Dealer wall poster, "Signs of the Times," showing an array of posters that would be available in a floor bin from which the customer would choose, Hip Products, Chicago, 40" h. x 28" w., c. 1967, very rare, $200-350.

Wall poster, "Poster World," Third Eye Inc., New York City, 29" h. x 19" w., c. 1967, common, $15-35.

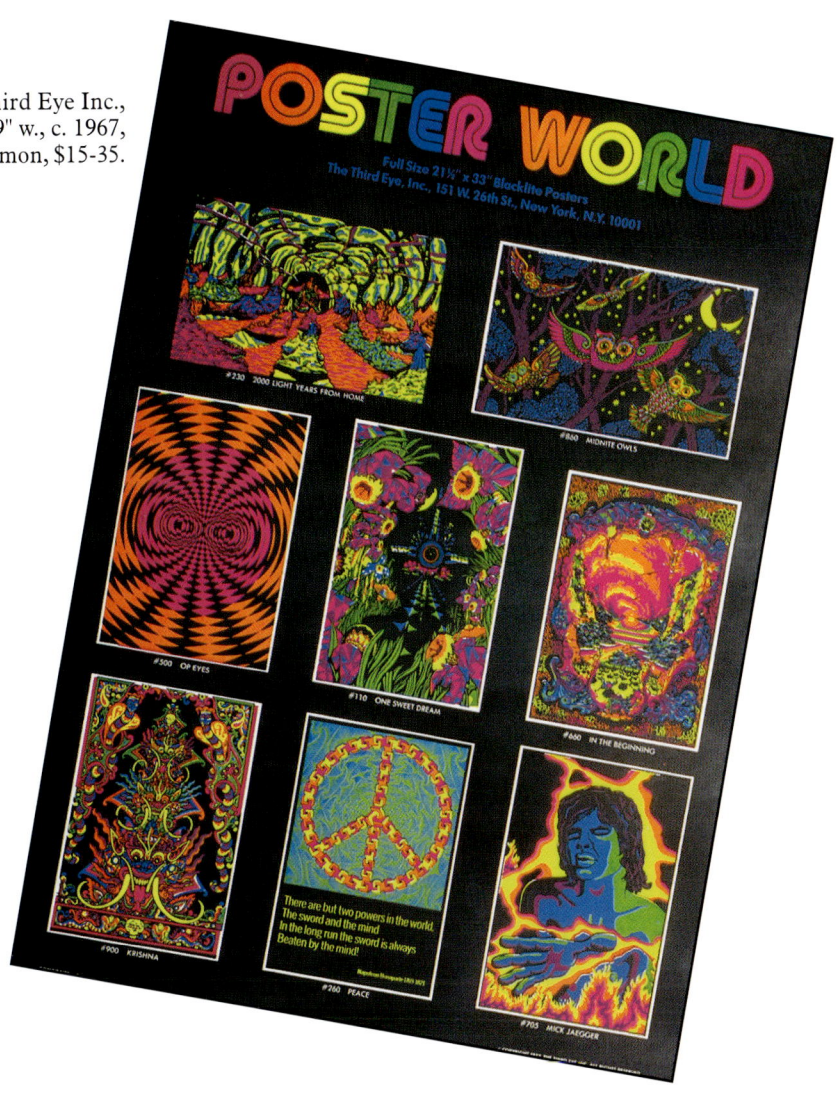

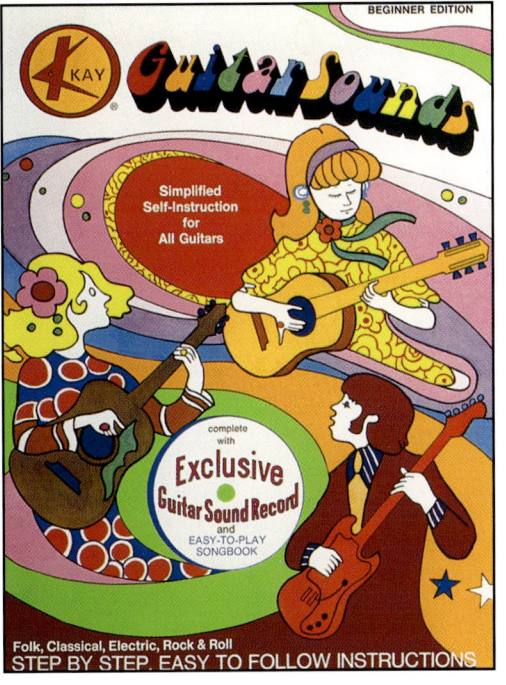

Guitar Sounds, rock guitar record and instruction booklet to accompany inexpensive starter guitar sold through stores, Kay Instrument Co., Chicago, 1970, uncommon, $15-35.

Poster "Tommy Toilet Sez," R. Crumb, Apex Novelties, San Francisco, 22" h. x 16" w., 1971, rare, $75-150.

"Crazy Decals," Heetrans, Inc, Pasadena, CA, " h. x 10" square, 1966, uncommon, $5-10 each.

Poster for head shop "Headquarters East," located in Cambridge MA, 34" h. x 26" w., common, $15-35.

From left: pinback, "I'm a Hippie" 3.5" dia., c. 1967, scarce, $20-45. *Courtesy of Gary Sohmers, Wex Rex Collectibles, Hudson, MA.*; pinback, "Sunshine Hippie," 1.25" dia., c. 1967, uncommon, $15-35.

Postcard, *The "Hashbury" scene*, E. F. Clements, San Francisco, c. 1968, common, $5-10.

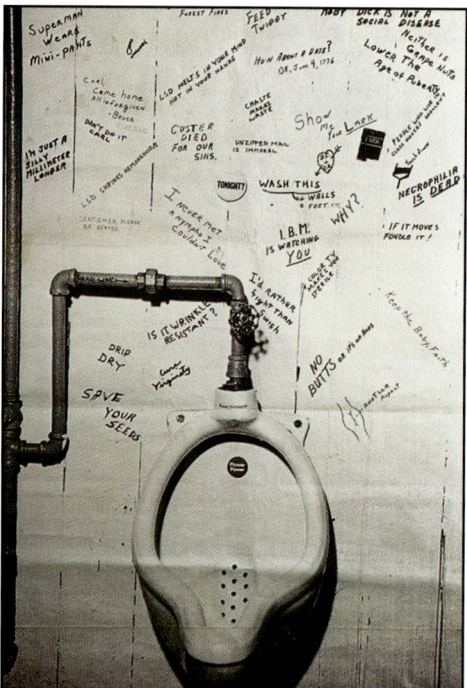

Urinal poster with hippie graffiti inscribed on wall, 28" h. x 20" w., c. 1967, uncommon, $15-35.

Psychedelic Buddha poster, 34" h. x 26" w., c. 1967, uncommon, $35-65.

Handbill for a head shop, "The Nothing Else," 110 Charles St., Boston, artist R. Hoyt, 11.5" h. x 8.5" w., c. 1967, uncommon, $25-45.

From left: counter top store display for leather jeans patches. Each patch sold for twenty-five cents in the late 1960's, scarce, $35-65; counter top store display, cardboard and foam in a VW beetle design, displayed multi-colored metal Flower Power Rings, 6" h. x 14" long, c. 1966, rare, $75-150, individual rings $5-10.

Postcard, "San Francisco Loves You," copyright Sea Cliff Press, San Francisco, 1967, uncommon, $5-15.

Counter top store display shows various hippie decals, c. 1967, individual decals, common, $2-3. *Courtesy of Gary Moise, 70's-store.com at Orange Trading Company, Orange, MA.*

Anti-war protest umbrella with hippie slogans and graphics. Words include No War, Easy Rider (popular cult movie with Peter Fonda, Dennis Hopper and Jack Nicholson), Hallo, Carnaby Street, Hippy, and Woodstock, cotton with wooden handle, made in Italy, 30," high, 1970, rare, $50-$125.

Top from left: turned wire necklace, common, price varies with intricacy of design and material, non-sterling $10-25, sterling or 925 Mexican silver $25-75; tea cups with mod design, c. 1967, uncommon, $5-15. *Bottom:* peace puzzle with box, "Love Burst" 1970, uncommon, $5-15.

Left: burlap wall hanging store display for displaying hair barrettes each with a different hippie symbol, uncommon, $35-65, individual barrettes $5-10. *Center:* leather hand tooled and painted shoulder bag, price varies with design, flowers are the most common, $15-35; various color suede fringed wrist and ankle cuffs, common, $5-10 each. *Right:* hanging store display with zodiac symbol leather hair barrettes, uncommon, $35-65 complete, individual barrettes $5-10 each. *Courtesy of Gary Moise, 70's-store.com at Orange Trading Company, Orange, MA.*

Hippie patches that attached by various methods—press-on, stic-on, and sew-on, c. 1967, uncommon, $5-15.

Left from top: beaded choker and necklace with American Indian motif, common, $10-25; plastic LOVE stash box, 5" h. x 9" w., c. 1968, uncommon, $15-35. *Center from top:* metal chain link belt with peace symbols, uncommon, $15-35; leather headband with attached metal peace symbol, common, $10-20; playing cards with psychedelic female face design, common, $5-10. *Right:* transistor radio with built-in pulsating psychedelic light display, made by Federal, 6" h. x 11" w., c. 1967, uncommon, $20-45.

Satirical paper napkin box set, "Politikins," 1970, uncommon, $10-20 per box.

Chapter Nine
Toys and Novelties

No part of American society was immune to the hippie movement. The youth market was a prime target for corporations to pander their goods as evidenced by the commercial use of hippie culture ideas used in toys that were sold to mainstream American children.

Harvey R. Ball of Worcester, Massachusetts, designed the Smiley Face in 1963 for which he was paid forty-five dollars by State Mutual Life Assurance Companies of America.[9]

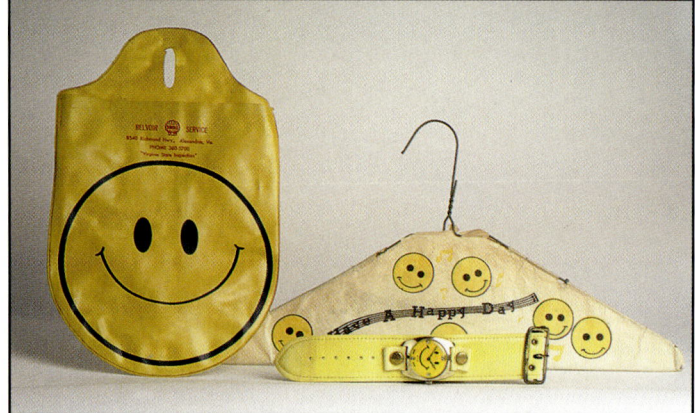

From left: Smiley Face vinyl wall pocket, 11" h. x 7" w., uncommon, c. 1968, $10-20; wire and paper Smiley Face clothes hangar, uncommon, $5-15; Smiley Face wristwatch with vinyl wrist band, A.T.C., scarce, $45-85.

Smiley Face transistor radio, box, and instructions, could be handheld with strap, or worn as a necklace, c. 1970, rare, $50-100.

From left: Smiley Face metal and leather chain link belt, 39" long, uncommon, $15-35; round metal smiley bank, 7" dia., c. 1966, uncommon, $25-50; Smiley alarm clock, Lux Time, Lebanon TN, 4" dia., common, c. 1968, $15-45; Smiley plastic wall clock, Emdeko, Lux Time, Lebanon TN, 7" dia., common, $15-45. *Rear:* clear vinyl floral Smiley Face handbag, 6" h. x 8" w., c. 1966, scarce, $45-85.

Composition hippy bank, 9" h. x 4" w., c. 1967, scarce, $50-100.

Agnew, Nixon and Mahareeshi Mahesh Yoga voodoo cloth doll, Psychedoll, 16" h. x 5" w., c. 1968, uncommon, $35-65 each.

Label and plastic bag with voodoo pin for the voodoo Psychedolls shown above.

Rock band cake topper, "The In Crowd," GN Papers, Inc., 1969, 15" h. x 11" w., c. 1968, scarce, $35-65.

Child's drum and cymbal set, rock band graphics, c. 1967, rare, $75-150.

Child's vinyl leather-look handbag, "Maddie Mod," Mego Corp., New York City, 11" h. x 9" w., 1970, scarce, $35-65.

From left: flower power do-it-yourself kit, "Penelope Pitstop," Larami Corp., Philadelphia, PA, 8" h. x 6.5" w. 1971, uncommon, $10-25; play shoes, plastic psychedelic design, Ray Plastic Inc., Winchendon Springs, MA, uncommon, $10-25.

Top: Psyche-Paths game, Funtastic, KMS Industries, 1969 common, $5-15. *Center from left:* fashion paint kit, "Brite and Wild Reflections," Artex, Lima, OH, uncommon, $15-35; school box with Peter Max-like graphics, Lebanon Packaging Corp., 7" h. x 10" w., c. 1968, scarce, $35-65. *Bottom from Left:* Comet psychedelic disk, Eagle Rubber Co., Ashland, OH, 10" dia., c. 1972, common, $10-20; psychedelic metal friction hot rod, Marx, 7" l. x 3.5" w., 1967, scarce, $50-100.

Inflatable hanging light bulb decoration, "Watt Turns You On", Dan-Dee Imports, New York, 1971, box 9" square, uncommon, $15-35.

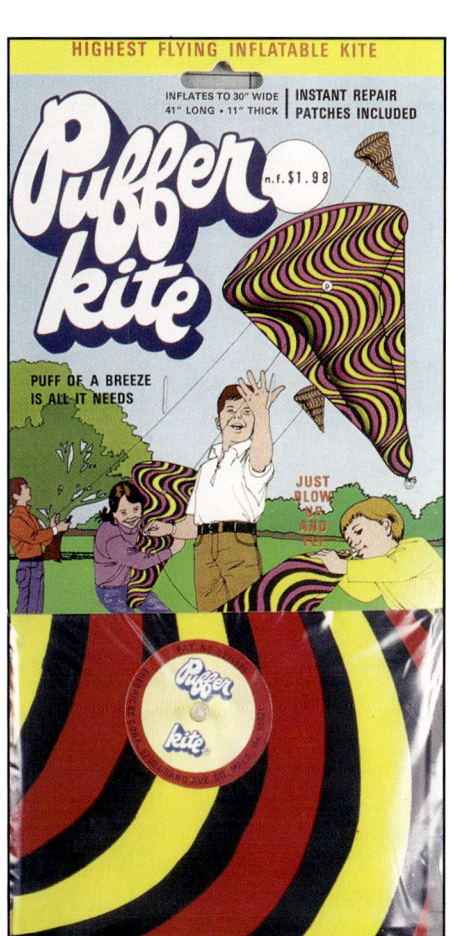

"Puffer Kite" with psychedelic optical illusion design, Fredericks Co., Minneapolis, MN, common, $10-20.

Pencil set with photo of hippie girl, "Up Tight," Reliance Pen and Pencil Corp., Lewisburg, TN, c. 1970, uncommon, $10-20.

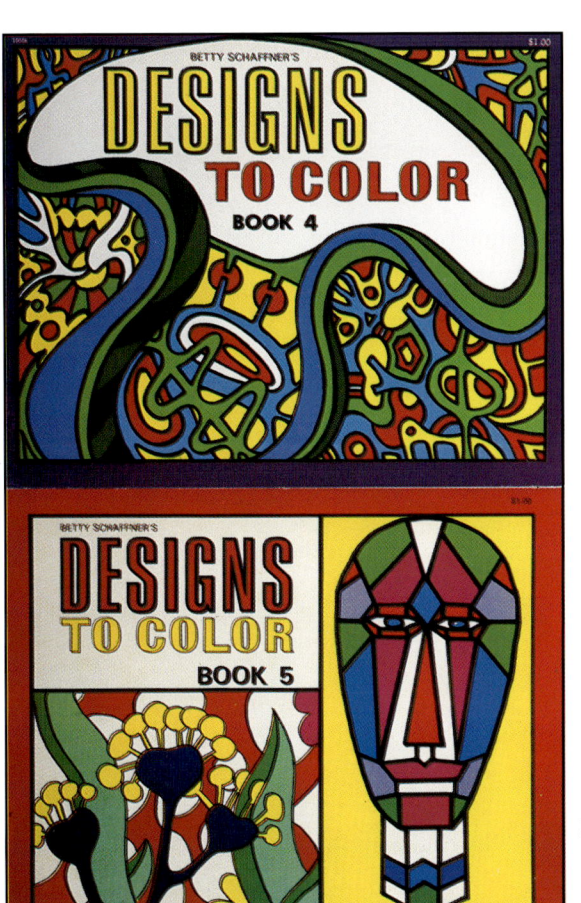

Six book set of psychedelic and mod designs "Designs to Color," 1967-70, uncommon, $5-10 per book.

From left: Rhonda rag doll with hippie symbols on both feet, Shindana Toys, 22" h. x 7" w. 1973, scarce, $35-65; pipe cleaner hippie doll, c. 1966, uncommon, $10-20; Gay Bob doll, copyright Harvey Rosenberg Inc., 12" h. x 1977, scarce, $150-300.

Top: Plastic model kit, "Drop Out Bus," Aurora, 8" long, 5" w., 1969, scarce, unbuilt with box $65-125; built without box lowers value by fifty percent. *Bottom from left:* plastic novelty, "Hippie Out House," 5.5" h. x 3" w., common, $5-15; plastic sand pail with hippie motif, Mammoth Plastics, Inc., Wellsburg, WV, 6" h. x 6" dia., scarce, $25-50; plastic novelty, featuring a hippie on a barrel, T.L., 6" h. x 2" w., common, $10-20.

Chalkware psycho-ceramic type figural banks, A. N. Brooks Corp., Merchandise Mart, Chicago, 10" h. x 5" w., 1971, scarce, $45-85.

From top: ceramic hippie couple salt and pepper shakers, Holt-Howard Inc., 2.5" high 1968, scarce, $20-45 pair; porcelain seated hippie couple, 3.5" h., scarce, $35-65 pair.

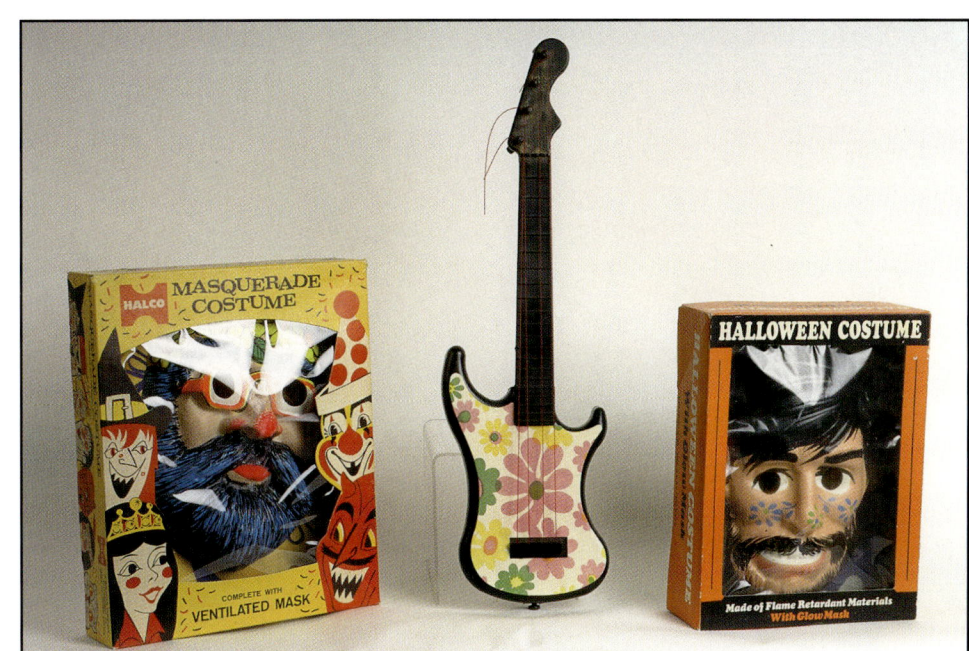

Right and left: hippie Halloween costumes, Halo, c. 1968, uncommon, $25-50; without box reduces value by fifty percent. *Center:* flower power plastic guitar, 18" h. x 5" w., Lapin Products, Asbury Park, NJ, 1972, uncommon, $15-35.

Mod water color set, Craft Master, 10" h. x 8" w., c. 1968, scarce, $45-85.

From left: model kit, "Flip Out," manufactured by Monogram, created by Stanley Mouse, who later became a well known San Francisco psychedelic rock poster artist, 9.5" h. x 5.5" w., 1965, scarce, unbuilt with box $50-100; model kit, "Surf Woody," hippie van, AMT, 5" h. x 9" w., c. 1968, scarce, unbuilt with box $75-150. For both models value is seventy-five percent less if built and without box.

From left: 33 1/3 LP album, *Rowan and Martin's Laugh-In*, Epic Records, common, $10-20; character mobile, *All in the Family*, copyright T.P.I, Lego, 1969, scarce, $35-65; doll, Flip Wilson as Geraldine, Shindana Corp., 1970, uncommon, $25-45; with box increases value by fifty percent.

Hippie Fun Wig, Topstone Rubber Co., Danbury, CT, c. 1973, common, $5-15 (post hippie period).

From left: Wacky Watches, Hassenfeld Bros., Pawtucket RI, 1968, uncommon, $20-45; Earth Beads, Larami Corp., Philadelphia, c. 1968, common, $5-10; Symbol Candle Kit with peace symbol and Smiley Face molds, Crafts by Whiting, 1972, uncommon, $15-35.

From left: Belt making kit, "Twist n' Weave," Crafts by Whiting, 1973, uncommon, $15-35; suede tassel belt, macramé kit, Hassenfeld Bros., Pawtucket RI, 1971, uncommon, $20-45.

Psychedelic *Crazy Daisys* plastic rings, c. 1967, uncommon, $10-20.

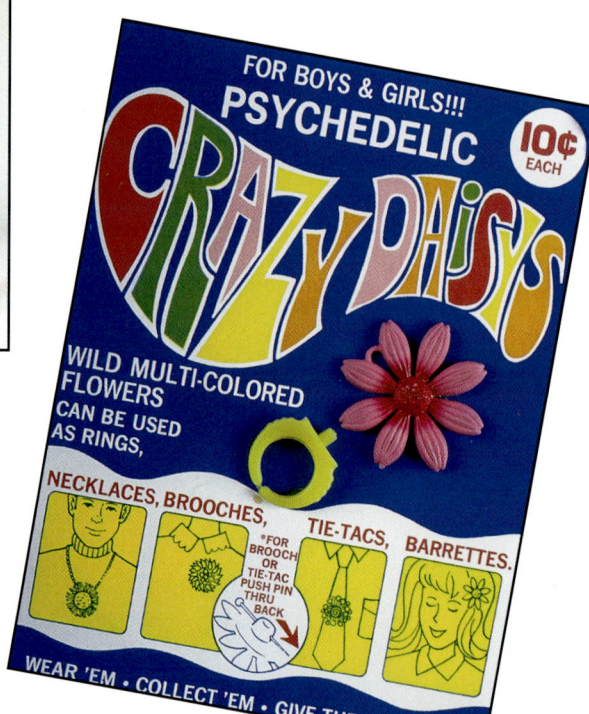

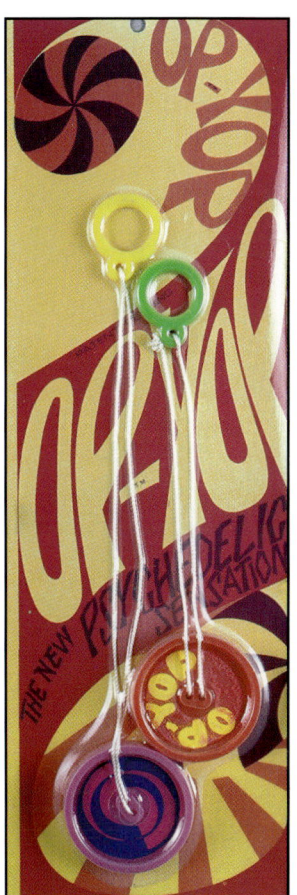

Op Yop toy, Kramer Designs, Madison Heights, WI, 14" h. x 4" w., 1968, rare, $45-85.

From left: "The Game of LOVE," Hassenfeld Bros., 1968, common, $10-20; "The World of Love" doll, Hasbro Industries, Pawtucket, RI, 1970, common, $25-50 in original box.

From left: "Hippy-sippy says" metal psychedelic pins, premium giveaway for soft candy beads found in western provinces of Canada in the late 1960's to early 1970's, 3/4" dia., 1969, uncommon, $5-$15; wooden push up standing hippie figure, one from a series of many different personalities, 5.5" high, 1968, uncommon, $10-$20. *Photograph courtesy of Walter "Hawkeye" Potaznick, West Bridgewater, MA.*

Medallion Kit, leather peace symbol, 12" high, 9" wide, Arrow Handicraft Corp., Chicago, IL, 1971, uncommon, $10-$25. *Photograph courtesy of Walter "Hawkeye" Potaznick, West Bridgewater, MA.*

Chapter Ten
Threads

Hippie apparel was quite colorful, festive and often hand made, an extension of the lifestyle. Clothes were regularly made from patches of leather or colorful cottons. Better-known leather craft shops included East West Musical Instruments Garment Company of San Francisco, North Beach Leather under the direction of Michael Hoban, and Walter Dyer in Boston. Custom designed leather pieces that cost $200-$300 thirty years ago, today command in excess of $500. A Janis Joplin type short leather jacket with hanging feathers from the arms and back sold recently for $375; a suede shirt with an embroidered cannabis leaf from East West Musical Garments sold for $500, and one of their custom designed appliquéd leather parrot jackets recently sold for $1,600.

Used leather jackets from the late 60s in good condition with whipstitching or tooled designs typically sell today for $100 to $200. An unusually designed leather belt with a silver hoop buckle, hand tooled peace signs and shooting stars recently sold for $135. Quite popular for woman today are the full-length embroidered wooly Afghan coats that typically range from $150 to $250. Other styles popularized by hippies included bell-bottoms, flared leg jeans and pants, peasant dresses, Afghan jackets, "Jesus" sandals, and folky embroidered tunic style shirts, Jessica McClintock Gunne Sax dresses, beaded and copper jewelry of Sarah Coventry, earth shoes designed by Anne Kalso, moghul and Nehru style jackets, batik and tie-dye. Colorful, psychedelic, sweeping paisley dresses by Emilio Pucci, and Mary Quant cosmetics from England were in vogue. Clothes were embellished with grommets, beads, rivets, studs and fringe.

Embroidered hippie tunic with original tag, modern version of the Hungarian peasant shirt, Sears, cotton, 1970, common, $15-45. Price varies with intricacy of embroidery.

Popular hippie and black power shirt with African origin, Dashiki, cotton, c. 1968, common design, $10-25.

Hot Pants, "Live Ins," rayon, c. 1968, uncommon, $15-35.

From left: tri-color mod design oversize-eyelet suede shoes with cork soles, made in USA, c. 1967, scarce, $35-65; knee-high suede Indian moccasin-style long fringe boots, uncommon, $25-50.

Suede jacket, moccasins and shoulder bag with matching American flag design, c. 1967, jacket, rare, $175-300; moccasins, scarce, $45-85; purse, scarce, $35-65.

Flower power shorts with rock band graphics (Fab Four knock-off image), cotton, c. 1968, rare, $75-150.

Poster, General Pants Co. advertising American flag design jeans, 34" h. x 22" w., 1971, scarce, $75-150.

Tie-dye dress, cotton, long, wide pointed collar and simple design, c. 1966, uncommon, $15-35; *The Complete Book of Tie-Dyeing*, Astrith Deyrup, Lancer Books, New York City, 1970, common, $5-10.

Smiley Face polka dot mod scarf, polyester, c. 1968, uncommon, $10-20.

From top: embossed metal bracelet with hippie symbols for peace, male, female, love, life, etc., c. 1968, scarce, $35-65; hammered metal necklace, coil and coke spoon design, uncommon, $20-45.

Hippie shirt, cotton, patchwork collar, wooden bead fringe, uncommon, $20-45.

Jessica McClintock Gunne Saxe, long prairie skirt, uncommon, c. 1968, $20-45.

Peace and love symbol shirt, cotton, c. 1967, scarce, $45-85; striped denim pants, c. 1966, uncommon, $25-50.

Peace symbol dress, cotton, scarce, $45-85.

Psychedelic design vest, cotton, uncommon, $20-45; patch pants, common, 1965, $10-25.

Leather sandals were a staple of the hippie outfit. The Mexican version of the popular "Jesus" sandal consisted of a sole that was cut out of a discarded automobile tire and two long overlapping pieces of rawhide sewn on the top. Called "huaraches" (pronounced wah-rah-cheese), they were initially amazingly stiff and uncomfortable, but once broken in would last for years. Bare Bottoms are a more sophisticated, fashionable offspring.

Bare Bottoms, unusual leather strap sandals, Eventoff Bros., Conshohocken, PA, 1967, rare, $50-100 with original box.

An assortment of hippie character bags. *Front from left:* faux fur bag, uncommon, $20-40; leather gypsy bag with braided shoulder strap, scarce, $45-85; leather hand tooled stash bag worn on belt, common, $10-25; hanging tassel stitch suede bag, uncommon, $25-50. *Rear from left:* vinyl flower power purse, uncommon, $15-35; hanging tassel stitch suede bag, uncommon, $25-50; American flag design purse, scarce, 35-65.

Suede western style fringe jacket, common, Sears, $25-65; similar jackets with better known designer labels range from $75-150. Suede floppy hat with braid, common, $10-25.

Shirt with various hippie faces, polyester, c. 1972, made in Mexico, scarce, $25-45; Faux suede bell bottoms, embroidered bird on guitar, Woodstock Festival symbol, one of many commercial items that capitalized on the historic rock concert's marketing appeal, c. 1971, scarce, $50-100.

Dashiki style shirt, cotton, c. 1968, uncommon design, $25-50.

Amoeboid design iridescent dress, polyester, uncommon, $25-50.

Rain jacket, psychedelic design, nylon, c. 1967, uncommon, $20-45.

An assortment of hippie character hats. *Front row from left:* biker hippie, scarce, $50-100; flower power hippie, uncommon, $15-35; Viet Nam Vet hippie, rare, $150-300; protest march hippie, scarce, $35-65. *Back row from left:* western hippie, common, $15-35; happening hippie, uncommon, $20-50; pull top beer can hat, very rare, $75-150; suede floppy hat, common, $10-25; farmer hippie, uncommon, $20-50.

Asian temple design dress with paisley print, cotton, Bleecker Designs, c. 1967, uncommon, $35-65. Name on label capitalizes on the well-known Greenwich Village street with many hippie shops.

Hippie slogan shirt, cotton, c. 1967, scarce, $35-65.

Sweatshirt, airbrushed Stanley Mouse signed design, c. 1965, rare, $150-300.

Psychedelic floral swirl design shirt, nylon, c. 1966, uncommon, $15-35.

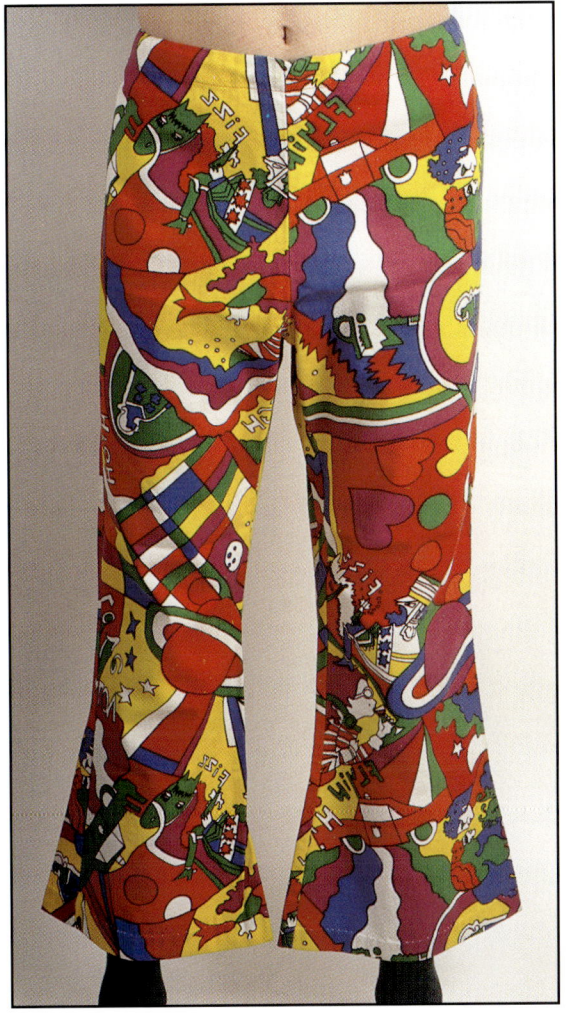

Bellbottoms, Peter Max-like design, cotton, c. 1969, scarce, $45-85.

From left: bead chain belt, Sarah Coventry, c. 1968, uncommon, $25-50; Mod Expo 70 wristwatch with moving flower center, 1970, scarce, $45-85.

Paisley sport coat, silk, c. 1967, uncommon, $50-100.

Suede floral zippered ponchos, made in Mexico, common, $25-50.

Fringed suede American-made pullover Indian style Poncho, actually worn at Woodstock Music Festival, August 1969 while Jimi Hendrix played the "Star Spangled Banner", the Who played "Summertime Blues", Crosby, Stills and Nash sang "Judy Blue Eyes", and Sly and the Family Stone sang "Take Me Higher" to nonstop rain and mud, 1969, rare, $100-200. Value is 50% less without Woodstock or similar provenance. Poncho pattern booklet, common, $5-15.

Left: Psychedelic pinwheel dress, polyester, c. 1967, uncommon, $25-50.

Right: Psychedelic bellbottoms, cotton, c. 1967, scarce, $35-65.

Hawaiian shirt with hippie symbols, cotton barkcloth, Rai Nani, 1966, scarce, $65-125.

Viet Nam advisors bush hat, 1965, rare, $150-300; Viet Nam tour jacket, embroidered lion patch, 1967, scarce, $100-200.

Mod psychedelic forest and mushroom dress, silk, c. 1968, scarce, $50-100.

Beaded cotton shirt, made in India, 1967, uncommon, $35-65.

Faux fur leopard coat, c. 1967, uncommon, $45-85.

Shirt with various hippie faces, cotton, made in USA, c. 1968, scarce, $35-65.

Dashiki style shirt-dress, heart pattern, cotton, uncommon, $25-50.

Mixed flower power style women's shirt, cotton, uncommon, $15-35.

Mod patent leather shoes, c. 1968, uncommon, $20-50. *Courtesy of Gary Moise, 70's-store.com at Orange Trading Company, Orange, MA.*

Mogul style overcoat, wool, uncommon, 25-50.

Psychedelic suit, polyester, c. 1967, common, $15-35.

Vinyl wristwatch band, American flag design, c. 1967, uncommon, $10-20.

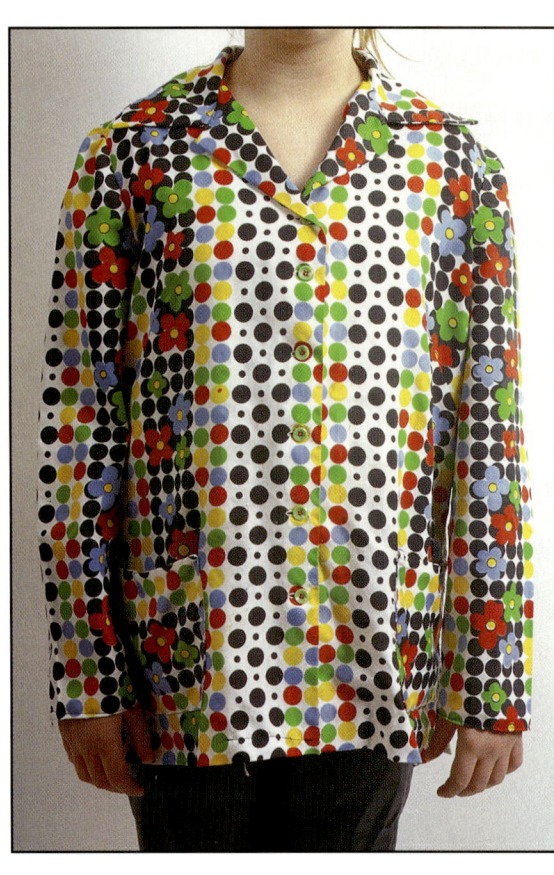

Mod flower power and polka dot shirt, cotton, uncommon, $15-35.

Dove and peace symbol dress, nylon, c. 1966, scarce, $45-85.

Long fringe suede vest, common, $15-30; value increases for vests with metal rings, embroidered or applied leather design.

Tie-dyed cotton shirt with Asian graphics and hieroglyphics, 1967, scarce, $35-65

Jacket with humorous hippie slogans and comic graphics, cotton, 1968, uncommon, $35-65. Similar images are found on household, novelty items and gum cards from the period.

Mod long sleeve shirt with the word "hippie" on shoulder yoke, rayon with matching rayon covered buttons, c. 1968, rare, $65-125.

Leather bellbottoms, East West Musical Instrument Co. Leather Garments, San Francisco, c. 1967, rare, $150-300.

Suede rock band shirt, applied leaf design, bell sleeves, East West Musical Instrument Co. Leather Garments, San Francisco, c. 1967, rare, $200-400.

Embossed East West Musical Instrument Co. Leather Garments patch, sewn into coats, jackets, shirts and pants.

From left: hippie headbands pattern pamphlet, 1970, Columbia-Minerva Corp., uncommon, $10-20; rainbow design fashion band, made by Goody, New York City, uncommon, $15-25.

Long sleeve psychedelic paisley shirt, nylon, c. 1967, common, $10-20.

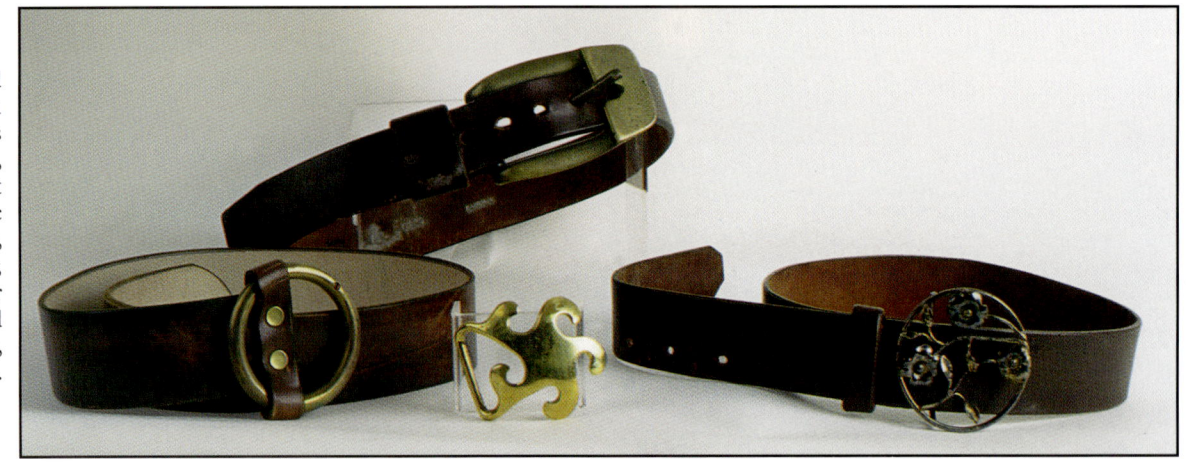

From left: wide hand tooled leather belts with large heavy brass buckles, 1966, common, $15-35; brass belt buckle with psychedelic wave design, Laurie, 1970, scarce, $25-50; hand made silver flower power belt buckle, hand tooled leather belt, 1967, scarce, $45-85.

Peter Max neckties, silk, c. 1968, scarce, $45-85 each.

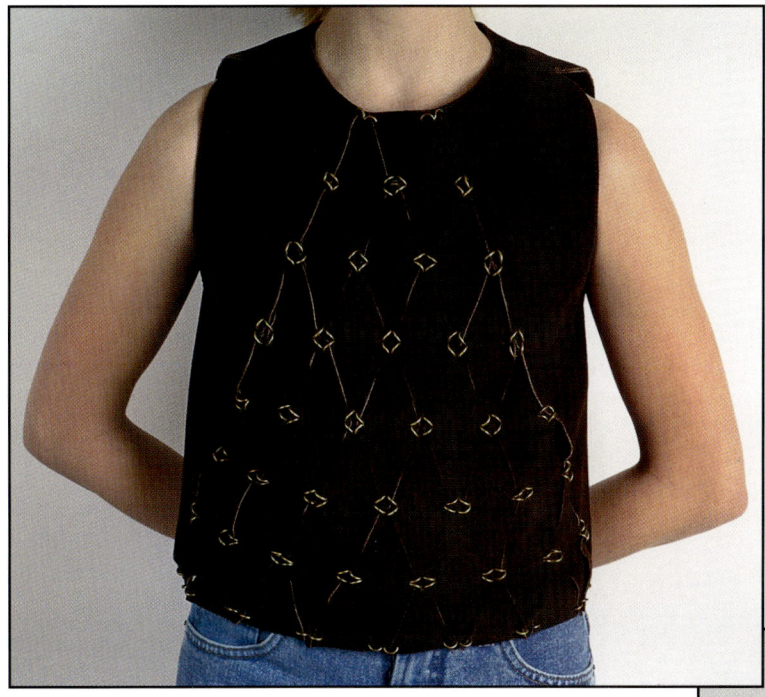

Suede vest; metal links create a diamond pattern, uncommon, $35-65.

Detail of leather gypsy bag with braided shoulder strap shown previously, scarce, $45-85.

From top: Hand tooled copper bracelet, c. 1968, common, $10-20; unusual intricately bent wire and stone necklace, scarce, c. 1966, $35-65; stamped metal links chain belt, Sarah Coventry, uncommon, $20-45. *Photograph courtesy of Walter "Hawkeye" Potaznick, West Bridgewater, MA.*

Robert Crumb in 1966 moved to San Francisco and soon after was considered one of the more successful underground cartoonists working in Haight-Ashbury. His artwork, often of a sexual and violent nature, satirically portrayed the American middle class. His Zap Comix attained cult-like status to a small segment of American youth. In 1967, he was asked by Janis Joplin and Big Brother and the Holding Company to design the cover for their *Cheap Thrills* record album.

Keep on Truckin' cloth patch, phrase popularized by underground comic artist R. Crumb, 1968, uncommon, $10-20. *Photograph courtesy of Walter "Hawkeye" Potaznick, West Bridgewater, MA.*

Stars and stripes, red, white, and blue suede vest with long fringe, c. 1967, scarce, $45-$85.

Chapter Eleven
Happenings and Concerts

Happenings were originally a blend of artistic performance that involved audience participation. However, many evolved into ill-defined music fetes where hallucinogenic drugs were central to what occurred. Streaking became a risky fad that involved running naked on stage or in the audience during an event, graduation, or concert. Many hippies chose to see Alexandro Jodorowsky's 1971 psychedelic Mexican western cult film classic, *El Topo*, while on LSD. They would then spend hours debating the film's symbolism and its significance to the meaning of life. Rumors of unusual happenings in Katmandu made this a destination for hippies seeking enlightenment, but similar experiences took place in many local parks across the country.

Before Bill Graham presented his series of rock concerts at the Fillmore Ballroom, he managed the San Francisco Mime Troupe, participants in many happenings. Concert promoters like Graham, along with Chét Helms, who started the family dog concert series at the Avalon Ballroom created an opportunity for psychedelic poster art to flourish. Collecting rock posters is a well-established and highly competitive field. Value depends on several factors that include: whether it is a first, second or third printing, the number of posters originally issued in each printing, the celebrity or the band and concert hall depicted in the poster, the desirability and appeal of the image, and the reputation and prominence of the graphic artist. First issues are quite rare, commanding prices into the high hundreds and even thousands of dollars, while second and third issues of popular posters often fetch in the low hundreds of dollars. Anyone interested in pursuing this area of collecting should purchase the reference books *The Art of Rock* by Paul Grushkin, Abbeville Press, 1987, and *The Collector's Guide to Psychedelic Rock Concert Posters, Postcards and Handbills* by Eric King, Svaha Press, 1996.

Hand screened rock concert poster on heavy cardboard stock, featuring The Velvet Underground, and The Freeborne, Boston Tea Party, 53 Berkeley St., Aug. 11-12, 1967, copyright Lightship Productions, 18" h. x 14" w., very rare, $800-1,500.

Lithographed rock concert poster on heavy paper stock, featuring Clear Light, and The Hallucinations, Crosstown Bus, 337 Washington St. Brighton, MA, artist J. McCracken, Aug. 25-26, 1967, Lightship Productions, 22" h. x 17" w., rare, $300-600.

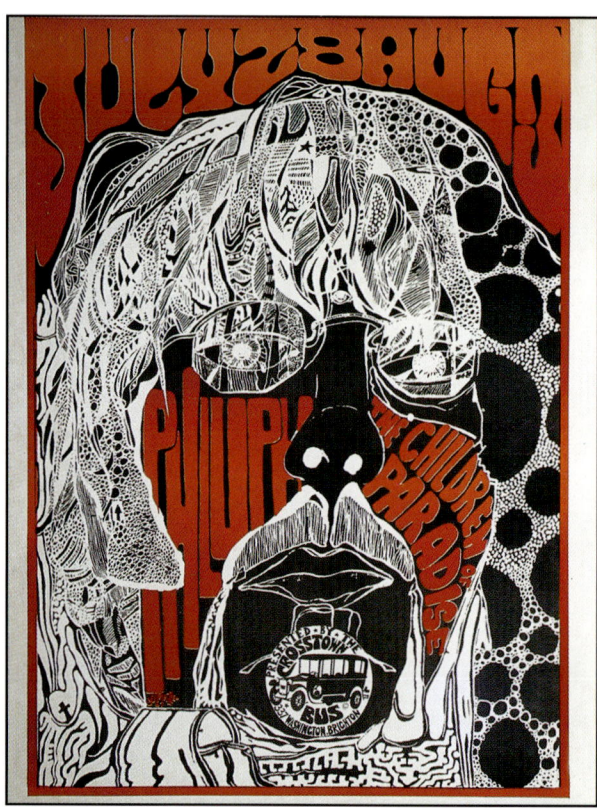

Hand screened rock concert poster on heavy cardboard stock, featuring Phluph, and The Children of Paradise, Crosstown Bus, July 28-Aug. 3, 1967, artist J. J. Mazzeo, 22" h. x 17" w., rare, $400-800.

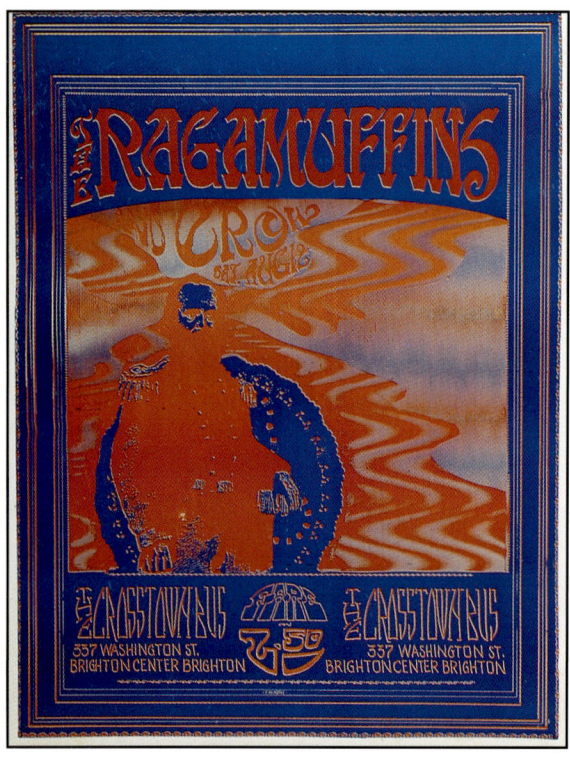

Lithographed rock concert poster on heavy paper stock, featuring The Ragamuffins, and Crow, Crosstown Bus, Aug 12, 1967, artist F. Murphy, 22" h. x 17" w., rare, $300-600.

Hand screened rock concert poster on heavy card board stock, featuring The Peanut Butter Conspiracy, and The 90th Congress, Boston Tea Party, July 14-15, 1967, copyright Lightship Productions, 20" h. x 14" w., very rare, $600-1000.

Lithographed rock concert poster on heavy card board stock, featuring Lothar and the Hand People, and The Street Choir, Crosstown Bus, Aug 4-5, 1967, artist J. McCraken, 22" h. x 18" w., rare, $300-600.

Lithographed rock concert poster on heavy paper stock, featuring Country Joe and the Fish, and Porpoise Mouth, Boston Tea Party, Aug. 25-26, 1967, 24" h. x 18" w., unsigned, rare, $300-600.

Hand screened rock concert poster on heavy paper stock, featuring The Peanut Butter Conspiracy, and The Bagatelle, Boston Tea Party, Aug 4-5, 1967, Lightship Productions, 20" h. x 16" w., rare, $400-800.

Lithographed rock concert poster on heavy paper stock, featuring The Group Image, The Clouds, Quicksilver Messenger Service, The Hallucinations, and The American Revolution, Boston Tea Party and WBCN 104.1 FM radio, June 6-8, 1967, and June 13-15, 1967, unsigned, 22" h. x 18" w., rare, $200-400.

Lithographed handbill on paper stock, featuring Lothar and the Hand People, and The Shakers, Boston Tea Party, June 30-July 1, 1967, artist F. Murphy, 10" h. x 8" w., uncommon, $25-50.

Lithographed handbill on paper stock, featuring Beacon Street Union, and Cloud, Boston Tea Party, July 25-27, 1967, 11" h. x 8" w., scarce, $100-200.

Dance concert handbill on paper stock, featuring Stack Summer, Orange (CA) YWCA, July 19, 6" h. x 4" w., scarce, $50-100.

The original location of the Woodstock Music and Arts Festival was to have been Walkill, New York. However, local townspeople enacted an ordinance to prevent the concert from occurring. From August 15-17, 1969, the three-day concert was held on Max Yasgar's six hundred acre dairy farm near the village of White Lake, the closest town to Bethel, New York. There were three deaths and two births during the rain drenched concert attended by nearly a half million people.

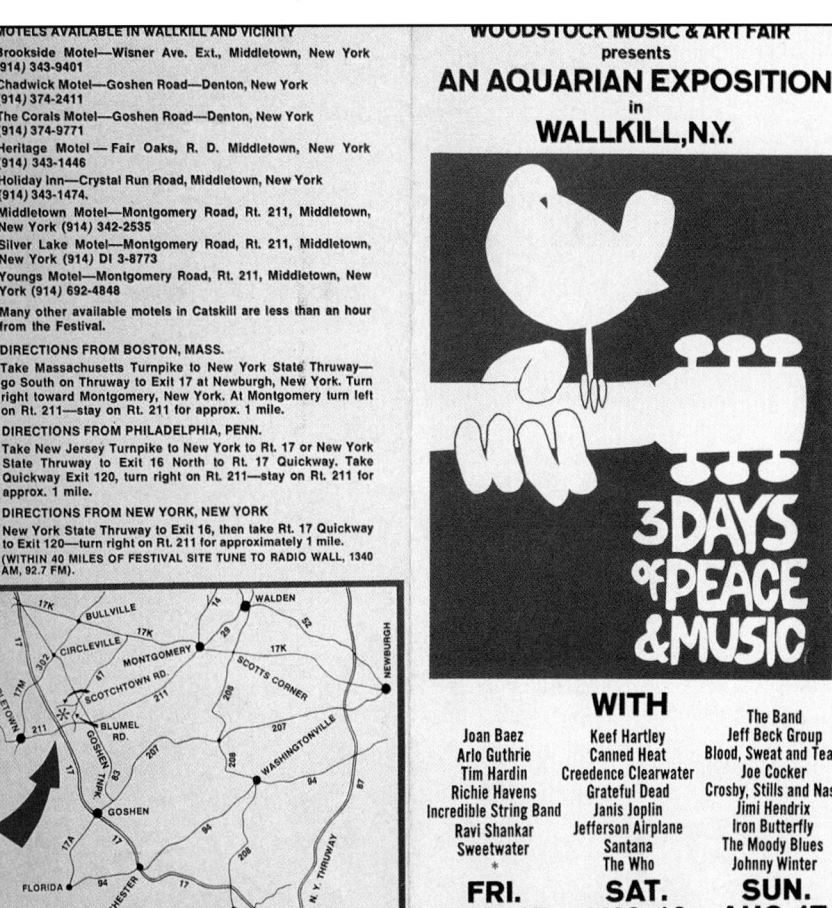

Mail brochure and ticket order form announcing the original site and dates of the Woodstock Music and Art Fair in Wallkill, NY, Spring 1969, 8" h. x 4" w. folded, very rare, $200-400.

Inside page of mail brochure advertising Woodstock Music and Art Fair.

The Haight-Ashbury Diggers and other political radicals organized the first "Human Be-In" held at Golden Gate Park in January 1967 to enlist grass roots support for their causes. Thousands of hippies attended a full day happening that featured gurus, rock music, and free love. The poster with a guru in a pyramid was created by two of the more popular artists, Stanley Mouse and Alton Kelley. It featured many of the San Francisco Rock Bands including The Grateful Dead, Jefferson Airplane, Quicksilver Messenger Service, Charlatans, Big Brother and the Holding Company, Country Joe and the Fish together with many radical leaders and poets including Timothy Leary, Allen Ginsburg, Michael McLure, Dick Gregory, and Richard Alpert (Baba Ram Dass). The occasion was a gathering of all the Hippie Tribes at Golden Gate Park Polo Fields in preparation for the "summer of love."

Poster, "A Gathering of the Tribes for a Human Be-In," artists Stanley Mouse and Alton Kelley, Jan. 14, 1967, Golden Gate Park, San Francisco, 20" h. x 14" w., $125-250.

Stick-ons, featuring the Bee Gees, Peppertree International, Inc, 11" h. x 8" w., 1969, uncommon, $25-45.

Lithographed rock festival poster, Jim Felt Presents, 1970 Portland Music and Art Fair, Oreg. Ltd., artist Michael James Strickland, 29" h. x 18" w., scarce, $100-250.

Pin-up wall posters, "Giant Groups Groove Out," Flip magazine staff, Kahn Communications Corp., 14" h. x 9" w., 1966, uncommon, $50-100.

Poster, "In God We Trust, All is OM," copyright Berkeley Bonaparte, 1967, P.O. Box 1250, Berkeley, CA, artist Rick Griffin, 20" h. x 14" w., uncommon, $65-125.

Poster, "Neon Rose #9," featuring The Wildfower, Matrix concert hall, Mar 3-5, 1967, Victor Moscoso, photo Elaine Mays, 20" h. x 14" w., uncommon, $50-150.

Concert poster, featuring Big Brother and the Holding Company, Quicksilver Messenger Service, and Congress of Wonders, Western Front #2, Grand Opening June 28-July 2, 895 O'Farrell, San Francisco, July 7-8, 1967, P.L. Co, 20" h. x 14" w., scarce, $75-150.

Concert poster, featuring Sandy Bull, and The Congress of Wonders, Western Front #3, San Francisco, July 7-8, 1967, artist Greg Irons, 20" h. x 14" w., scarce, $75-150.

Concert poster featuring Morning Glory, and Indian Head Peace Band, Dance Academy, Western Front, San Francisco Oct 13-14, 1967, artist John Thompson, 23" h. x 13" w., scarce, $75-150.

Concert poster, featuring Nick Gravenitis and The Congress of Wonders, Matrix, 3138 Fillmore in the Marina, San Francisco, Nov 8-13, 1966, artist R. Garbell, 22" h. x 14" w., scarce, $100-200.

"Sparta Poster #2," Dave Schiller 1967, San Jose, Ca, suggested retail price $1.00, artist J. Michaelson, Sparta Graphics, 22" h. x 17" w., common, $15-35.

Early psychedelic LP record albums. *Front from left: 13th Floor Elevators*, International Artists, 1966, rare, $100-300; *West Coast Pop Art Experimental Band*, scarce, $50-100. *Rear from left: Jimmy Hendrix Experience*, Reprise, uncommon, $25-50. Mothers of Invention with Frank Zappa, *Freak Out*, Verve, uncommon, $45-85.

Early psychedelic LP record albums. *From left: Love*, 1966, Elektra, uncommon, $25-50; *Jefferson Airplane Takes Off*, RCA Victor, 1966, common, $10-20; *Pearls Before Swine*, ESP-Disk, uncommon, $25-50.

From left: Ne Hezaz Ut, Qualiton, Hungarian, rare, $100-300. Obscure garage albums of the late 60s and early 70s and European psychedelic rock bands are quite scarce and very aggressively sought after. *Boston Tea Party*, Sidewalk Productions, MGM Records, scarce, $45-85; Strawberry Alarm Clock, *Incense and Peppermints*, Universal City Records, uncommon, $25-50.

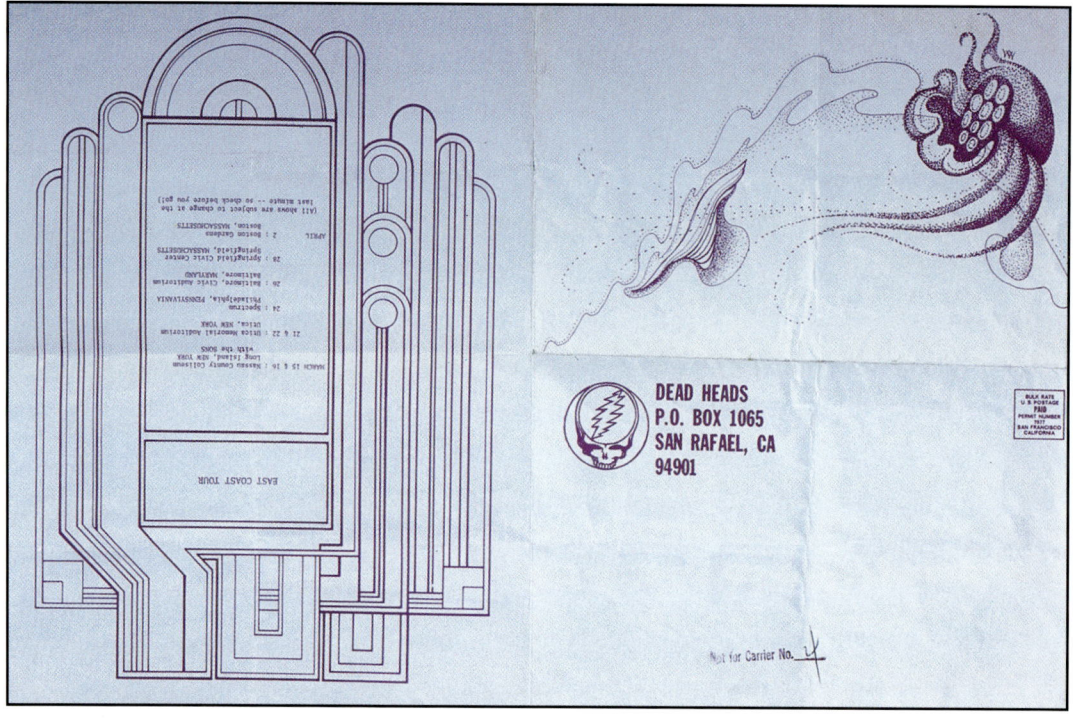

Newsletter, *Dead Heads*, mailed to fans of the Grateful Dead for announcements and upcoming concerts, c. 1972, uncommon, $15-35.

Movie pressbook for *The Love-Ins*, Columbia Pictures, 17" h. x 11" w. 1967, uncommon, $10-25.

Concert program for 1971-72 Chicago area events, Triangle Productions Inc., uncommon, $35-65.

*T*he *Committee* was originally a play shown in theatres such as San Francisco's North Beach Night Club. It was quite risqué and on occasion was halted and the actors arrested for "lewd and dissolute conduct in a public place" because of the obscene language and oral sex scene that took place on stage.

One sheet movie poster advertising *The Committee*, a movie that is "anti-everything." Commonwealth United, originally a San Francisco and Los Angeles theatre production, 1969, common, $10-25.

One sheet movie poster advertising *Head*, starring the Monkees, Columbia Pictures, 1969, scarce, $125-175.

Poster advertising a "Popcorn Happening," benefit and performance for children under 12, sponsored by Singing Mothers LSD Relief Society Studio, 621-1944, 21" h. x 14" w., scarce, 1966, $50-125.

Quasars ice cream poster, 919a Cole St. near Carl in the Haight, for the after hours munchies crowd, artist G. Roberts, 22" h. x 14" w., scarce, 1966, $45-85; identical 5" x 7" handbill is common, $5-15.

Poster, Robie Basho with the Contraceptive, Joyful Wisdom Enterprises, 14" h. x 8" w., scarce, 1966, $35-65.

"Health and the Family" handbill, Haight-Ashbury, and University of California Community Forum, 11" h. x 8" w., 1966, scarce, $15-35.

Chapter Twelve
Underground Press

Bi-monthly magazine, *Paperbag*, v1 n1, Feb., 1968, published by MPS Corp., Los Angeles, CA, 11" h. x 8" w., uncommon, $15-35.

Underground papers and books were to be found in hundreds of cities and college towns throughout the country. The first West Coast underground paper was the *Los Angeles Free Press*, started in 1964. This was followed by *The San Francisco Oracle* and *The Berkeley Barb*. *The Berkeley Barb* claimed a circulation of ninety thousand at its peak in 1969. On the East Coast, the *East Village Other* started in 1965. *The Village Voice* and *Rat* (which later became *Women's Liberation*) were two of New York's better known papers. All of these papers reported on antiwar and free speech demonstrations, local rock events, the social and political scene among the downtrodden, and included articles on drugs and other counterculture happenings.

The Liberation News Service was started in 1967 during the height of the Vietnam War by political revolutionaries Raymond Mungo and Marshall Bloom. This underground press service regularly supplied articles, photographs and cartoons to over one hundred underground newspapers and nearly a million readers. It eventually split up along political lines; one group went to a commune in Western Massachusetts with all the money, while the other, composed of Marxists, remained in New York. Both continued to supply news stories.

Another essential component of the 1960s underground press were psychedelic authors like Herman Hesse, Carlos Castaneda, and R.D. Laing who wrote about their experiences with drugs and the search for meaning in life.

Monthly magazine, *Sexology*, v34 n6, January 1968, published by Sexology Corp., New York City, 7.5" h. x 5" w., uncommon, $5-10.

Paperback, *Hippies, Hindus and Rock n' Roll*, copyright Bob Larson, McCook, NE, 90 pages, 1969, uncommon, $10-25.

Weapons for Counterinsurgency, published by NARMIC (National Action Research on the Military Industrial Complex), January 15, 1970, 101 pages, 11" h. x 8.5" w., scarce, $50-100.

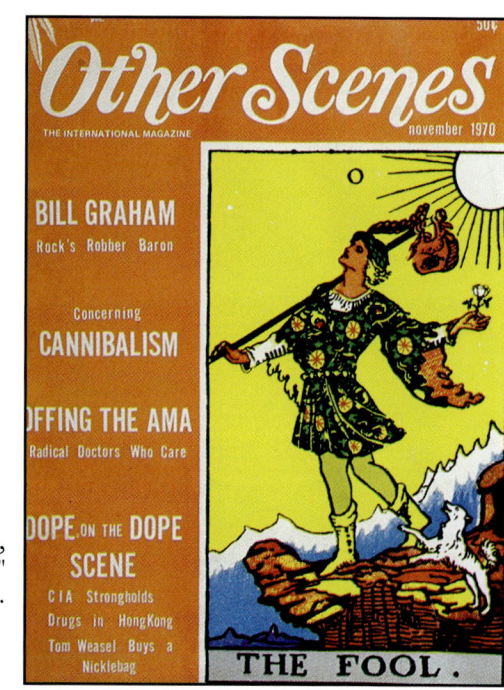

Journal of hip and alternative lifestyles, *Other Scenes*, v4 n9, November, 1970, published monthly by Other Scenes, Inc., 11" h. x 8" w., common, $5-15.

The birth control pill was introduced to American society during the 1960s. This was probably the most prominent medical advancement to facilitate the "free love explosion" that was an essential element of the hippie lifestyle.

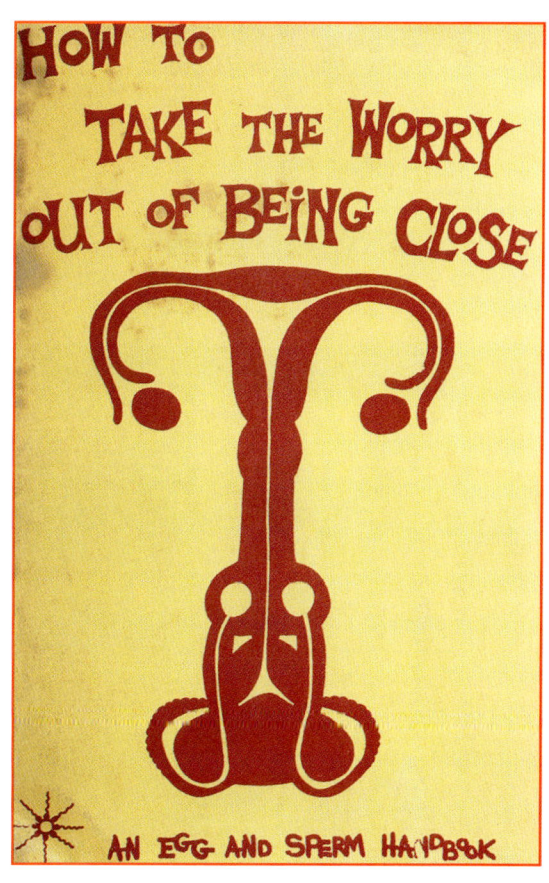

How to Take the Worry Out of Being Close, An Egg and Sperm Handbook, by Marian Johnson Gray and Roger Gray, contraception, abortion, birth control and the pill, 32 pages, 8.5" h. x 5.5" w., 1971, scarce, $35-65.

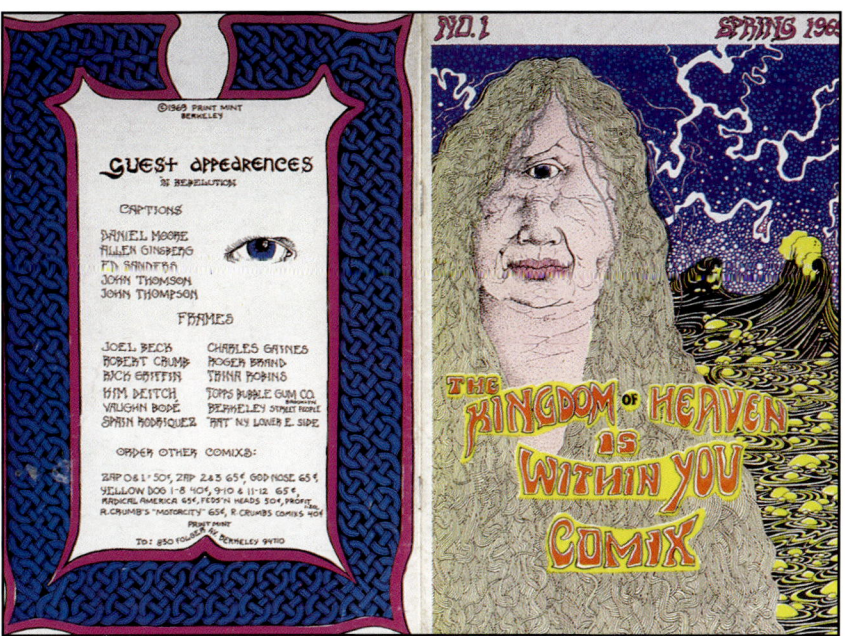

Underground comic book, *The Kingdom of Heaven Is Within You Comix*, No. 1, Spring 1969, published by Print Mint, Berkeley, CA, 9.5" h. x 6.5" w., uncommon, $10-25.

Chicago area underground paper, *Seed*, v5 n8, June 6, 1970, 17" h. x 12" w., common, $10-35; price varies with cover image and content.

Crawdaddy, The Magazine of Rock n' Roll, No. 6, November 1966, editor Paul Williams, 11" h. x 8.5" w. Early issues were hand stapled and mimeographed, scarce, $45-85.

The description in the credits of *The Santa Fe Hips Voice* states that this is "A hippie-type newspaper, sometimes called an underground magazine, we appeal to hard core dissidents, effete intellectuals, impudent snobs, thinking people, teeny boppers, straights, heads, tourists, gays and other assorted cool individuals."

The *Santa Fe Hips Voice*, #12, Wednesday August 26, 1970, published bi-monthly, scarce, $10-35.

Monthly magazine, *Freak Out, USA*, no. 2, February, 1967, Warren Publishing Co., New York City, 50 pages, 11" h. x 8" w., common, $5-20.

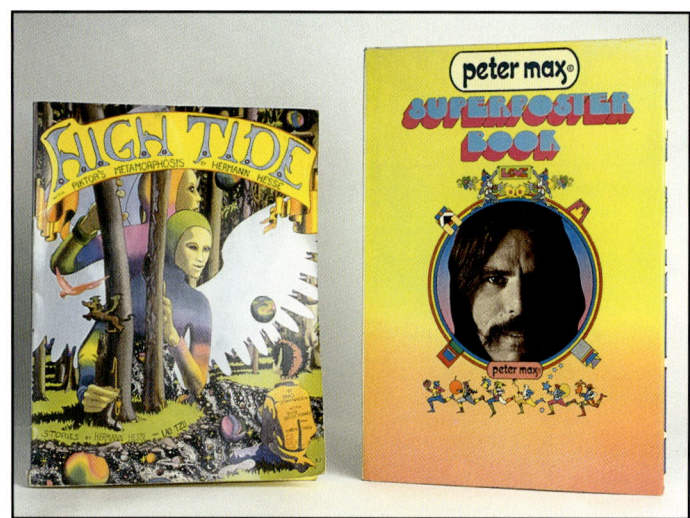

From left: *High Tide: With Picktor's Metamorphosis* by Hermann Hesse, Harmony Books, 1972, soft cover, scarce, $35-65; hardcover, rare, $75-150. Right: *Peter Max Super Poster Book*, Crown Publishers, New York, 16" h. x 11" w. 1971, soft cover, uncommon, $35-65; hardcover, scarce, $65-125.

Bi-monthly magazine, *Win, Peace and Freedom thru Nonviolent Action*, published by the War Resisters League, New York City, 24 pages, 10.5" h. x 8" w., 1968, uncommon, $5-15.

The Oracle was considered one of the most important and influential underground papers from Haight-Ashbury. Started by Allen Cohen in a joint venture with psychedelic entrepreneur, Ron Thelin, the first issue was published in September 1966. Known for its psychedelic front page artwork, the *Oracle's* goal in the words of Cohen was "to judo the tabloid low price anguish propaganda and profit form to confront its readers with a rainbow of beauty and words ringing with truth and transcendence." A complete list of all the underground papers produced in the country during the hippie period would be quite difficult to achieve, however some of the more successful papers include:

OB Peoples Rag, San Diego
The Door, San Diego
St. Louis Outlaw
St. Louis New Times
Washington Free Press
San Francisco Oracle
S.F. Express Times
S.F. Good Times
Berkeley Barb
Berkeley Tribe
Phoenix, Boston
Avatar, Boston
The Bridge, Chicago
The East Village Other, New York City
Village Voice, New York City
Columbus Free Press, Columbus, Ohio
The Daily Planet, Chicago Northside and Miami, FL
The Seed, Chicago, IL
The Rat Subterranean News, New York City
Winter Soldier (Viet Nam Veterans Against the War)
Los Angeles Free Press
The Sun, Detroit, MI
Kaleidoscope, Milwaukee and Madison, WI
Haight Ashbury Tribune
Guerilla, Detroit, MI
King Bee Comix
The Sunday Paper
Zygote
Frendz, United Kingdom
Logos, Montreal
Changes, New York City

Quicksilver Times, Washington, D.C.
The Great Speckled Bird, Atlanta, GA
Helix, Seattle, WA
Open City, Los Angeles, CA
The Paper, Venice, CA
Creem, Los Angeles
Dragonfire, Kent, OH
Joint Issue, Lansing, MI (Michigan State University)
The Paper, East Lansing, MI
Rag, Austin, TX
Free Press, Vancouver, B.C.
Georgia Straight
Old Mole, Bost, MA
Great Swamp Erie Dada Boom, Cleveland, OH
Fifth Estate, Detroit, MI
International Times, United Kingdom
All You Can Eat, New Brunswick, NJ
Mojo Navigator R & R News, San Francisco, CA
Iconoclastic Magazine, Austin, TX
Haight-Ashbury Maverick
Open City, Los Angeles, CA
The Flash, Pasadena, CA
The Movement
The Free Venice Beachhead
Provo
The Minneapolis Flag
This Is Happening
Tuesday's Child
The Puget Sound Partisan

Oracle, v1 n1, November, 1968. San Francisco area underground paper published monthly "dedicated to the brotherhood of man and the peace of the world." 14" h. x 11" w., inaugural issue scarce, $45-85; successive issues common, $10-30.

Underground music industry paper, *The Beat*, v3 n12, August 26, 1967, Hollywood, CA, 14" h. x 11" w., uncommon, $10-25.

Magazine, *Ikon*, v1 n3, July 4, 1967, published bi-monthly, New York City, 11" h. x 8.5" w., scarce, $35-65.

Peter Max Magazine, No. 1, 1970, published quarterly, by Peter-Lee Inc., New York City, 12" h. x 9" w., scarce, $45-85.

Magazine, *New Times*, v1 n1, April 8, 1970, E-M Publishing Corp., New York City, 14" h. x 10" w., scarce, $20-45.

Underground newspaper, *Fish Cheer*, No. 7, April 23, 1971, Pensacola, FL, 12 pages, 16" h. x 11" w., scarce, $15-45.

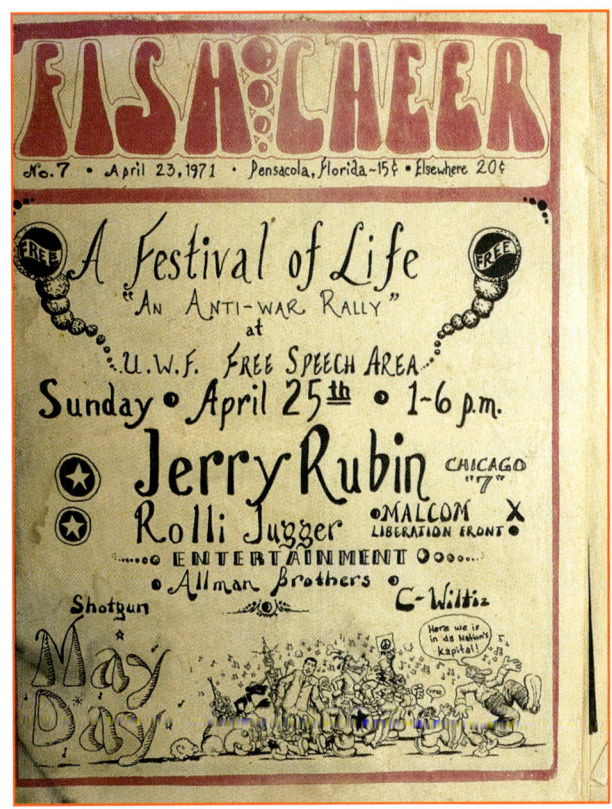

Radical anarchist propaganda booklet, *Outlaws of Amerika, Communiques from the Weather Underground*, July 1971, published by The Liberated Guardian, New York City, 48 pages, 7.5" h. x 5" w., rare, $75-150.

1969 summer catalogue, *Heliotrope*, cover by Thomas Wier, San Francisco, uncommon, $15-35.

What's Happenin', v1 n1, June 1, 1967, 8 page paper distributed by radio station KJRB Spokane, Washington, 23" h. x 15" w., scarce, $15-35.

Graffiti, v1 n6, December, 1967, published by R.S.V.P. (Redeeming Social Value Publisher), New York City, 34 pages, 8.5" h. x 7" w., scarce, $20-45.

San Francisco Express Times, v2 n2, January 14, 1969, 15 pages, 16" h. x 11.5" w., common, $5-15.

Rising Up Angry, v1 n1, July, 1969, Chicago, IL, 20 page paper featuring reports on grass roots movements in America, 17" h. x 11" w., scarce, $35-65.

The Word, v1 n1, May, 1969, Boston, MA, 17" h. x 11.5" w., uncommon, $5-15.

Forty-eight page booklet, *Hippies-Hypocrisy and "Happiness"*, published by Ambassador College Press, Pasadena, CA, 1968, 8" h. x 5" w., uncommon, $15-35.

First page of *Hippies-Hypocrisy and "Happiness"*, expressing conservative anti-hippie sentiment.

Jann Wenner, a student in San Francisco, founded *Rolling Stone Magazine* in 1967. Initially a one-page broadsheet, it quickly grew into the biggest, most influential of all rock magazines. It became a huge national success with many interviews of the biggest stars in rock n' roll.

Rolling Stone, No. 43, October 4, 1969, the longest surviving and most successful underground paper of the period, common, $10-20, early issues scarce, $25-75.

Avant Guard, no. 3, May 1968, 64 pages, 11" square, common, $10-20. Inside back page of this issue announced "a call for entries for an international poster competition based on the theme: No More War!" One of the winners is shown in chapter one of this book.

Bi-monthly publication, *The Westwood Village Square*, no. 1, Spring, 1968, 11" square, uncommon, $15-35.

Bi-weekly underground paper, *Changes*, v2 n3, April 1, 1970, Lenny Bruce cover, New York City, 14" h. x 11" w., uncommon, $10-25.

Booklet, *Groovy is…*, written by Roland Swanson, illustrated by Walt Scott, Hallmark Cards, Inc., 1971, 5.5" h. x 4" w., uncommon, $15-35.

Inside pages from *Groovy is…*, hippie period "pop wisdom".

Treason! quarterly of the Free School of New York, winter, 1968, Che Guevera cover, 11" h. x 8.5" w., scarce, $35-65.

Life, special edition, Woodstock Music Festival, 1969, common, $10-20.

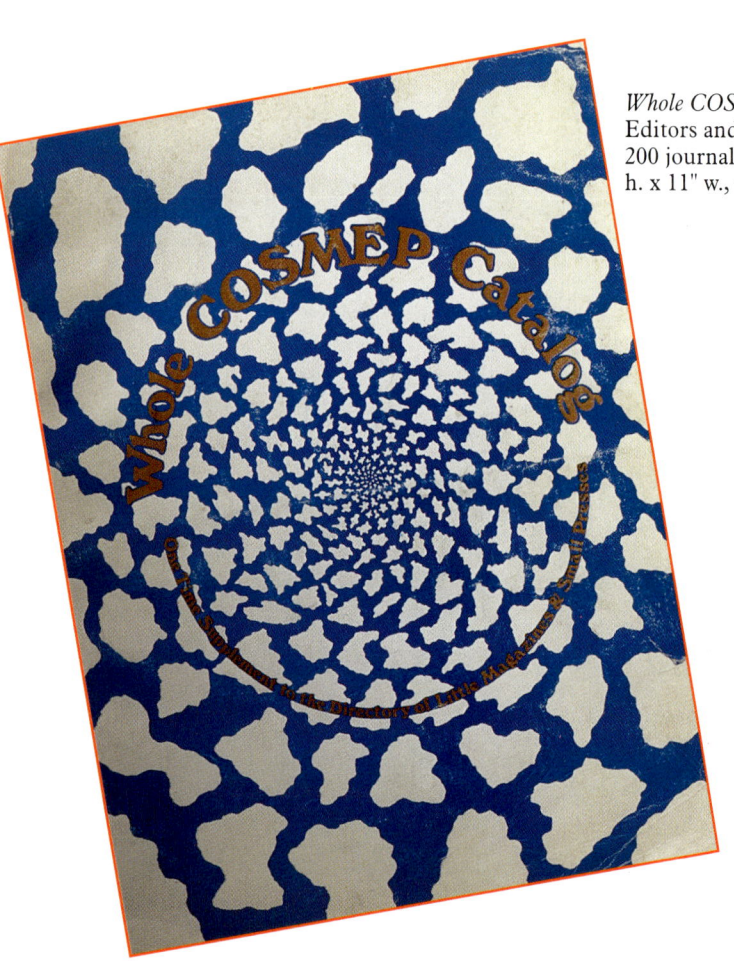

Whole COSMEP Catalogue, (Committee of Small Magazine Editors and Publishers Inc.) includes one sample page from over 200 journals and publishers of the underground press, 1973, 14" h. x 11" w., very rare, $75-150.

Amerika, v1 n1, a student magazine distributed free to 180 universities, published at the University of Chicago, copyright Mark Braverman, 15" h. x 11" w., scarce, $15-45. *Photograph courtesy of Walter "Hawkeye" Potaznick, West Bridgewater, MA.*

A NATIONAL PUBLICATION / NEW YORK / FEBRUARY 1, 1969 / 25¢

Guardian

independent radical newsweekly

Old Glory still waves at San Francisco State College, thanks to adhesive tape & police clubs. Nearly 500 arrested. Page 3.

the Ally

A NEWSPAPER FOR SERVICEMEN

No. 12 DECEMBER 1968 FREE to GIs Box 9276 Berkeley, Calif.

GI Resistance Escalates

Presidio murder sparks GI protest

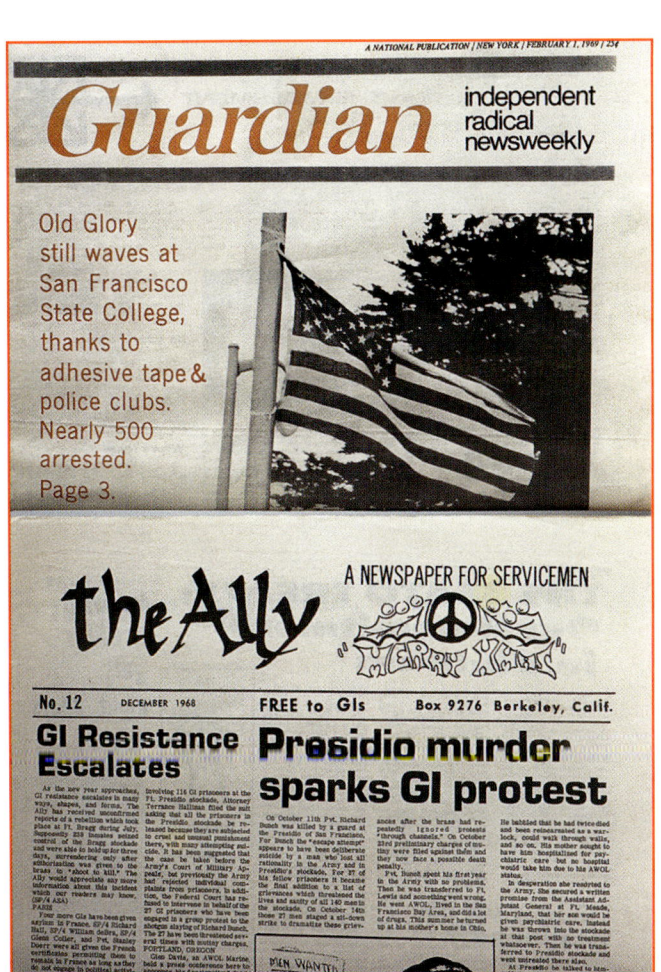

From top: Guardian, independent radical newsweekly, February 1, 1969, New York, 16" h. x 11" w., common, $5-15; *The Ally, A Newspaper for Servicemen*, No. 12, December 1968, articles and advice for soldiers opposed to the war, 16" h. x 11" w., uncommon, $10-25.

Various cause related and counter culture paperback books. *Top from left: From the Movement Toward Revolution*, by Bruce Franklin, 1971, published by Van Nostrand Reinhold, New York City, scarce, $25-50; Three ring binder with protest slogans, uncommon, $15-35; *Vote Power, The Official Activist Campaigner's Handbook*, 1970 by the Movement for a New Congress (Palmer Hall, Princeton, NJ) published by Prentice Hall, Englewood Cliffs, NJ, scarce, $35-65. *Bottom from left: A Journal of Female Liberation*, issue 2, February 1969, Cambridge, MA, scarce, $25-50; *No Bosses Here, A Manual on Working Collectively*, published by Vocations for Social Change, Cambridge, MA, uncommon, $15-35; *Do It! Scenarios of the Revolution*, by Jerry Rubin, 1970, copyright Social Education Foundation, published by Simon and Schuster, New York City, common, $5-10.

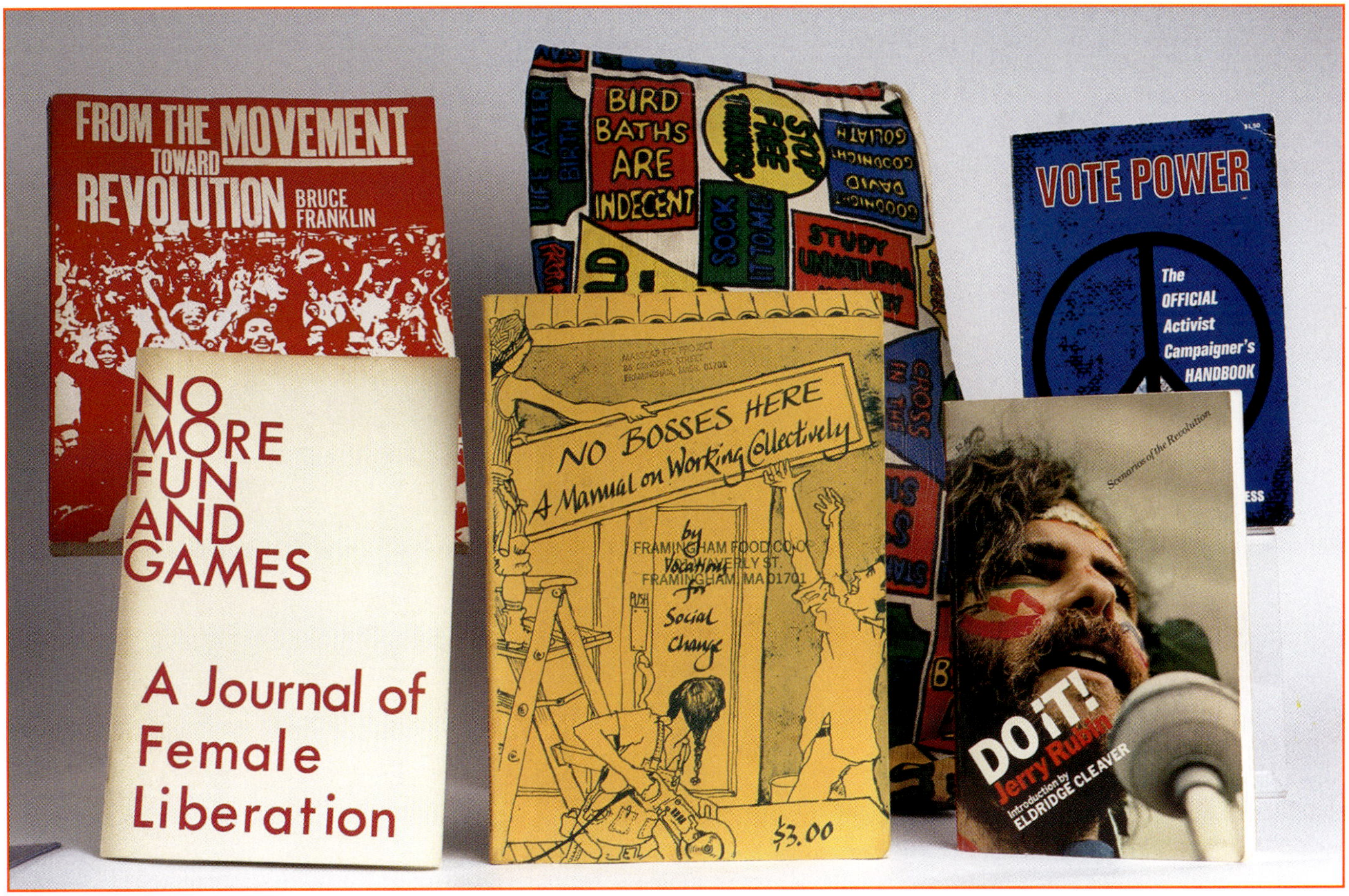

Like many of the important hippie writers, Lawrence Ferlinghetti was originally a 1950s Beat writer whose popularity continued throughout the 1960s and beyond. His poetry reflected the changing times and found an eager audience among the new hippies. Some of his most popular titles include *Assassination Raga*, about the assassination of Robert Kennedy, *Bickford's Buddha*, about attempting to attain a Buddhist's perfect vision, and *Through the Looking Glass*, about ingesting LSD on a flight to India.

From left: Beat It, Kid…You Can't Vote!, compiled by Harvey Kurtzman, Fawcett Publications Inc., Greenwich, CT, 1967, 5" h. x 8" w., common, $5-15; *Shots, Photographs From The Underground Press*, David Fenton, The Liberation News Service, 1971, 11" h. x 8" w., uncommon, $15-30; *Tyrannus Nix*, by Lawrence Ferlinghetti, New Directions Publishing Corp., New York City, 1969, 5" h. x 8" w., common, $5-15.

A selection of paperbacks and magazines on various hippie lifestyles from the late 1960's. *Center: The Hippy's Handbook, How to Live On Love*, Ruth Bronsteen, Canyon Books, New York City, 62 pages, personal accounts and obscure information on hippie lifestyle, 8.5" h. x 5.5" w., rare, $65-125. *Upper right: The Hippie Cookbook*, common, $10-15. *Lower left: Bad America*, discount coupon book for trendy hippie stores in metro Boston, 1969, rare, $35-65.

[1] Stevens, Jay, *Storming Heaven: LSD and the American Dream*, Harper & Row, 1987.

[2] Helfman, Elizabeth, *Signs and Symbols Around the World*, 1967

[3] Nunan, R., Personal communication, April 24, 2002.

[4] Brown, Patricia Leigh, *New York Times*, December 16, 1999.

[5] Cowan, Paul, *Only Yesterday*, Warner Books, New York, 1990, pp. 6 and 7.

[6] Kirkpatrick Sales, *SDS*, Vintage Books, 1974

[7] Solis-Cohen, Lita, "Flags Fly High at Americana Sale", *Maine Antique Digest*, July, 2002, p. 24-E.

[8] Cowan, Paul, *Only Yesterday*, Warner Books, New York, 1990, p. 105

[9] www.smileycollector.com/smileytrivia.htm

Barnes, Carolyn. *The Hippie Scene*. New York, NY: Scholastic Book Service, 1968.

Cowan, Paul. *Only Yesterday*. New York, NY: Warner Books, 1990.

Landy, Eugene. *The Underground Dictionary*. New York, NY: Simon and Schuster, 1971.

White, Suzanne. *Psychedelic Collectibles of the 1960's & 1970's*. Radnor, PA: Wallace-Homestead, 1990.

Wolfe, Burton. *The Hippies*. New York, NY: Signet Books, 1968.

Zahler, Kathy, and Diane Zahler. *Test Your Countercultural Literacy*, New York, NY: Simon and Schuster, Inc., 1989.

A selection of common paperbacks and journals on hippie drug culture from the late 1960's, $5-20.

A selection of uncommon paperbacks on various hippie topics from the late 1960's, $10-35.

Saturday Evening Post weekly magazine from 1967 with cover stories on hippie culture, common, $10-20.

Fusion, a magazine of the music world from California, 1971, uncommon, $10-25.